CAMBRIDGE LIBRARY COLLECTION

Books of enduring scholarly value

Religion

For centuries, scripture and theology were the focus of prodigious amounts of scholarship and publishing, dominated in the English-speaking world by the work of Protestant Christians. Enlightenment philosophy and science, anthropology, ethnology and the colonial experience all brought new perspectives, lively debates and heated controversies to the study of religion and its role in the world, many of which continue to this day. This series explores the editing and interpretation of religious texts, the history of religious ideas and institutions, and not least the encounter between religion and science.

George Fox's 'Book of Miracles'

George Fox (1624–91), founder of The Religious Society of Friends (or Quakers), was well known during his lifetime as a healer and worker of miracles. He wrote prolifically of how he used God's power to effect over one hundred and fifty cures, of both physical disease or injury and mental or psychological problems. This work was critical to spreading the word about Quakerism in its early years. Many of Fox's papers were lost after his death, but from the clues and fragments that remained, and a contemporary index of his works, Henry Cadbury (1883–1974) was able to create this book, published in 1948. The preface makes clear that this was not intended as a work of critical analysis, though the findings are annotated with historical and documentary detail. The editor's devotion to his task is testament to the historical and spiritual significance of Fox's contribution to Quakerism.

Cambridge University Press has long been a pioneer in the reissuing of out-of-print titles from its own backlist, producing digital reprints of books that are still sought after by scholars and students but could not be reprinted economically using traditional technology. The Cambridge Library Collection extends this activity to a wider range of books which are still of importance to researchers and professionals, either for the source material they contain, or as landmarks in the history of their academic discipline.

Drawing from the world-renowned collections in the Cambridge University Library and other partner libraries, and guided by the advice of experts in each subject area, Cambridge University Press is using state-of-the-art scanning machines in its own Printing House to capture the content of each book selected for inclusion. The files are processed to give a consistently clear, crisp image, and the books finished to the high quality standard for which the Press is recognised around the world. The latest print-on-demand technology ensures that the books will remain available indefinitely, and that orders for single or multiple copies can quickly be supplied.

The Cambridge Library Collection brings back to life books of enduring scholarly value (including out-of-copyright works originally issued by other publishers) across a wide range of disciplines in the humanities and social sciences and in science and technology.

George Fox's 'Book of Miracles'

GEORGE FOX
EDITED BY
HENRY JOEL CADBURY

CAMBRIDGE
UNIVERSITY PRESS

CAMBRIDGE UNIVERSITY PRESS

Cambridge, New York, Melbourne, Madrid, Cape Town,
Singapore, São Paolo, Delhi, Mexico City

Published in the United States of America by Cambridge University Press, New York

www.cambridge.org
Information on this title: www.cambridge.org/9781108045032

© in this compilation Cambridge University Press 2012

This edition first published 1948
This digitally printed version 2012

ISBN 978-1-108-04503-2 Paperback

GEORGE FOX'S
'BOOK OF MIRACLES'

The true and lively Pourtraicture of Valentine Greatrakes Esq.
of Affane in y. County of Waterford, in y. Kingdome of Ireland.
famous for curing several Deseases and distempers

I. Valentine Greatrakes, the 'Touch Doctor'

(*See* page 73)

GEORGE FOX'S
'BOOK OF MIRACLES'

EDITED WITH
AN INTRODUCTION AND NOTES
BY

HENRY J. CADBURY

WITH A FOREWORD BY
RUFUS M. JONES

CAMBRIDGE
AT THE UNIVERSITY PRESS
1948

Printed in Great Britain at the University Press, Cambridge
(Brooke Crutchley, University Printer)
and published by the Cambridge University Press
(Cambridge, and Bentley House, London)

Agents for U.S.A., Canada, and India: Macmillan

CONTENTS

ILLUSTRATIONS

[1] There are two other miniatures by the same artist of the same subject, one at Devonshire House dated 1653, and one at Montagu House. All three are reproduced in S. R. Gardiner's *Oliver Cromwell* (1899), opposite page 168, on page 69, and opposite page 160, respectively.

FOREWORD

By RUFUS M. JONES

During his researches in Friends Library in Friends House, London, in 1932, Henry Cadbury discovered a comprehensive Catalogue of all papers and books written by George Fox, collected shortly after his death. In the Catalogue list of important lost books is a 'Book of Miracles'. Though the 'Book' itself is lost the interesting Catalogue cites the beginning and ending words of the account of each miracle. There are more than 150 entries of cures attributed to Fox, many of them of the seeming miracle type of cure. Many of the cures can be reconstructed, and the 'Book' here produced gives the names of many persons cured, the type of disease or accident, and many of the details of the cures. It is a unique piece of critical reconstruction work of a very high order and makes it possible for us to follow George Fox as he went about his seventeenth-century world, not only preaching his fresh messages of life and power, but as a remarkable healer of diseases with the undoubted reputation of miracle-worker. The early editors of his writings saw fit to tone down this aspect of the great founder of Quakerism and the 'Book of Miracles' was not printed with the *Journal* and the other writings that have come down to us. Now for the first time the general reader will be able to realize to what an extent George Fox had the vogue in his day of being a miracle-worker, and it consequently gives us, in some degree, a *new* George Fox.

It is peculiarly interesting historically for the light it throws on the way in which the spiritual 'father' of the Children of Light in this particular met the needs and the expectations of 'the Seekers' who formed the central nucleus of the early Society of Friends, and of their fore-runners on the Continent. For 100 years there had been a succession of spiritual reformers who had proclaimed the inward Light, the inward Word and the Divine seed, but who had felt compelled to content themselves with an invisible Church, composed of unorganized believers scattered over the world, because no one had yet appeared with apostolic authority to set up a visible Church which would restore the pure primitive Church of the apostolic times, and which would, they believed, under the leadership of the invisible Christ as its Head, become the one and universal Church of the ages. This long-hoped-for man with apostolic power would of necessity, they all believed, prove his apostolic power by signs and evidences by which the original apostles established their claims to leadership, namely the performance of miracles.

Sebastian Franck (1499–1542) was one of the first in the period of the Reformation to set forth with clarity and vigour the type of invisible Church with its inward Word which he believed would take the place temporarily of both of the visible churches of his time. But he pointed out in his *Chronica* that 'some desire to allow Baptism and other ceremonies to remain in abeyance *till God gives another command and sends out true labourers into his harvest.* Some have a great desire and longing for this.' Franck does not specifically say that 'the true laborers' with 'the new command' will verify their commission with miracles, but he implies it, and many of his successors positively state that miracles will be the true sanction of the apostolic commission.

Henry Barrowe, in his book, *A Brief Discovery of the False Church* (1590), is one of the earliest writers to make Franck's implication perfectly explicit. He says that there can be no true Church and no authentic ministry or sacraments 'until some second John the Baptist, or new apostles, be sent from heaven, except peradventure they, after their long travail, bring forth some new Evangelist; and surely if they make a new ministrie they must also make a new gospel *and confirm it with miracles*'.

The Dutch scholar, Dirck Coornhert (b. 1522) is the spiritual 'father' of the 'seeker-movement' in Holland, known as 'the Collegiants'. Coornhert saw no hope of a true visible Church in his time and he proposed an *interim Church*, while 'waiting' for God to set up the authentic Church. Coornhert's followers, who formed the Dutch Collegiant groups of Seekers, definitely looked for a heaven-sent apostolic founder who would prove his commission by miracles. This expectation is explicitly put in a vivid way by the Collegiant leader of Amsterdam, Galenus Abrahams, who asserted that 'Nobody nowadays can be accepted as a messenger of God unless he confirms his doctrine by miracles'.

This was essentially the position of the English 'Seekers'. William Allen in his book, *A Doubt Resolved or Satisfaction for the Seekers* (1655), says:

> They [the Seekers] make a considerable obstacle in their way of coming into Church-communion, Gospel ordinances, viz. *the want of a right administrator*, for they suppose that since that general apostacy from the purity of faith and Gospel Order which befell the Churches, upon the entering of the Papacie into the world, *there hath none appeared sufficiently authorized by God* to rally again what has been routed by the hand of the enemy...and that therefore we must be content to *wait* until God shall raise up some such, whose authority in this behalf *He shall attest with visible signs of His presence, by Gifts of the Holy Ghost, and divers miracles as at the first erection of Gospel Churches.*

Further evidences could be produced if it were necessary to indicate that the atmosphere, in George Fox's formative years, was charged with the expectation of the coming of an apostolic founder of the true Church, and that this founder would attest his commission by authentic gifts and miracles. For 100 years there had been 'quiet persons in the land', belonging in heart and spirit to the invisible Church, but waiting and seeking for someone authorized by God and endowed with gifts by Christ to be the beginner of a new apostolic Church with Pentecostal Spirit and Power. George Fox's 'Book of Miracles' must be read in the light of this historical background and the reader will have no difficulty in seeing that Henry Cadbury has rendered a notable service in showing how completely George Fox fitted into the historical situation which his spiritual forerunners had prepared for him.

There are two further points that call for brief consideration: (1) the factual aspect in these miracle accounts, and (2) the modern psychological interpretation of these types of healing.

I think the reports of healing, of sudden cures, as George Fox reported them, are substantially trustworthy. There can be no doubt that he was a dedicated lover of truth and intended to report exactly what happened. But it is an unescapable fact that every person, however honest and morally qualified he may be, tends to enhance in the reporting, in the telling, a story that has a large element of the mysterious, the seemingly miraculous, about it, and especially if it carries a strong emotional tone. I have myself found it necessary to stop telling certain striking incidents, for I caught myself *improving* them with the repeated telling. The startling accounts in the chronicles of saints and mystics are usually heightened, but that need not imply fraud. The reporters may have been quite honest, they may very well have been doing only what is quite unavoidable in telling of mysterious happenings, especially if often repeated. We may allow, therefore, for some unconscious heightening of the miraculous in these accounts of George Fox, but I have no doubt that the healings are in the main trustworthy.

We now know through our psychological studies what a very large factor a faith attitude, an expectant state of mind, plays in the preservation and in the recovery of health. There seem to be almost no limits to the curative effects of suggestive faith and emotional expectation. The shrines at Lourdes in France and at Saint Anne's in Quebec have furnished vivid demonstrations of this principle and numerous Protestant faith-healers and prayer-healers have added their impressive testimony.

We have been slowly but effectively discovering what an enormous role the endocrine glands of the body play in these sudden curative processes. They are immediately responsive to emotional states of mind and they suddenly pour their internal secretions, especially the adrenals, into the blood, which thereupon carries powerful explosive forces—internal TNT—to all parts of the body, with extraordinary transforming effects. Psychological laboratories, for instance, report cases of persons who in the highly suggestible state of hypnosis, when there are no inhibitions, have raised an actual blister under a postage stamp on their back when it was suggested to them that it was a fly-blister.

Certain persons appear from time to time in history who possess in a high degree this peculiar capacity of awakening faith and of carrying suggestive attitudes irresistibly into action. George Fox was in his day unquestionably a person of that type. He awakened faith in minds that were prepared for his way of life and thought, and they 'believed in his belief'. There are many instances, given in his *Journal*, of the curative power of faith over his own body. Here is a characteristic instance of this power:

> There was in the company a mason, a professor, but a rude fellow, who with his walking rulestaff gave me a blow with all his might just over the back of my hand, as it was stretched out; with which blow my hand was so bruised and my arm so benumbed, that I could not draw it to me again. Some of the people cried, 'He hath spoiled his hand for ever having the use of it any more'. But I looked at it in the love of God (for I was in the love of God to all that persecuted me) and after a while the Lord's power sprang through me, and through my hand and arm, so that in a moment I recovered strength in my hand and arm in the sight of them all.[1]

This curative power, which surged through his own body when he looked at his arm with complete faith and in the love of God, he set into operation effectively in the lives of persons who came under his unique influence. There are occasional references to a peculiar power in his eyes and there is no mistaking the suggestive sway of his personal

[1] *Cambridge Journal*, Vol. I, p. 133.

influence in awakening faith. William Penn testifies that he never saw George Fox when he was 'not a match for every service or occasion'. I think we can take it as settled that the cures and remedial effects actually occurred substantially as reported. Whether they should be classed as 'miracles' is another matter. In any case they throw much light on the dynamic personality of George Fox.

PREFACE

This book owes its inception to a Fellowship in Quaker Research which I held at Woodbrooke Settlement, Selly Oak, Birmingham, for two terms in 1932–3. Thereby I had opportunity to study in detail the ponderous manuscript Catalogue of George Fox's Papers (of which I published a partial edition in 1939) and to discover in its index an index to the lost 'Book of Miracles'. Part of the cost of preparing the present work for the press was defrayed by a grant from the Milton Fund of Harvard University. Part of the cost of publication has been met by a grant of Philadelphia Monthly Meeting of Friends from the Rebecca White bequest for printing and distributing the writings of George Fox and Robert Barclay. To those responsible for each of these forms of assistance I wish to express my gratitude.

The preparation of the book has extended with interruptions over many years, but I hope no serious inconsistencies have resulted from this long and intermittent process. During all this time I have received the generous help of many libraries and librarians. I mention especially the staffs of the library at Friends House, London, and of the Quaker Collection at Haverford College, Pennsylvania.

At a time when all publication is difficult, the Cambridge University Press has been willing to meet my hope that this book would be undertaken by them to match in outward form and in high-grade publishing skill their earlier production in 1911 and 1925 of the journals of George Fox as edited by Norman Penney in three volumes.

I have not attempted to explain or to evaluate the material here collected, but have tried to set down objectively the text of the records and their historical context. No doubt others will wish to study and to interpret this material in its relation to religion, to psychology, and to medicine in general and to such special fields as Quakerism,

Preface

Seventeenth Century England, faith healing, folklore, and 'enthusiasm'. I am, however, grateful to Rufus Jones for the illuminating foreword which he has contributed. More than that, he has been for half a century an inspiration toward the practice of Quakerism as well as to the study of its history.

Three English Friends of the older generation have put all students of George Fox in debt to them—William Charles Braithwaite (1862–1922), Norman Penney (1858–1933), and A. Neave Brayshaw (1861–1940). To their memory this volume is dedicated.

HENRY J. CADBURY

CAMBRIDGE, MASSACHUSETTS

December 1947

INTRODUCTION

MIRACLE IN SEVENTEENTH-CENTURY ENGLAND

The importance of miracle in the history of religion is well known. A survey of religions both of civilized and of uncivilized man reveals few if any from which the belief in miracles is absent. Especially of miracles of healing do accounts come to us from nearly all peoples and religions. Not only in Christianity from the earliest times until now, but also in ancient Egypt, Greece, Rome, India, China and Japan, in the religions of Judaism, Buddhism, Zoroastrianism and Islam have occurred episodes which even to contemporaries have seemed to be miraculous cures.[1] Though the method of description has often shown marked similarity in the various records, this is not due to a literary dependence that would throw doubt upon the independent origin and credibility of the events narrated. It is inevitable that such stories whenever told should follow a natural technique of presentation.

The environment of the early Quaker movement and its own inner enthusiasm were well suited for the growth of a belief in miracles. The assurance of the sects that the powers of the apostolic age were being manifested in them led to a confidence in their contemporary ability to prophesy and to work cures. William Prynne in 1645 accuses the sectaries, and in particular Captain Paul Hobson, of 'boasting of working miracles and casting devils out of men possessed by their exorcismes, as the Jesuists and Papists doe'.[2] Among the errors listed in 1646 by Edwards in his *Gangraena* was the power to work miracles.[3]

[1] Cf. C. J. Wright, *Miracle in History and in Modern Thought* (1930), pp. 64 ff., 130–41.

[2] *A Fresh Discovery of some Prodigious Wandring—Blasing—Stars & Firebrands, Stiling themselves New-Lights, etc.* p. 13.

[3] Part I, Error no. 145, p. 32. Cf. the specific instances of such claims, p. 66 (Anabaptists healing the sick with the anointing of oil), p. 136 (Kiffin's cure of a woman by the same means), p. 213 (Henry Denne's cure of a gentlewoman near Canterbury of an incurable disease, by means of dipping).

Introduction

Mathew Coker, whose tracts were published in 1654, was a notable instance of one who claimed to have worked miracles, and his claims were accepted by no less orthodox a person than Robert Gell, D.D., Rector of St Mary, Aldermanbury.[1] One of his tracts is *A Short and Plain Narrative of Matthew Coker . . . in reference to his Gift of Healing which is here clearly evidenced in several remarkable instances*. A little later in his *Whip of Small Cords to Scourge Antichrist* he argues that although miracles abated by division from Rome, yet he and his contemporaries could claim according to the measure of grace the gifts of the Apostles' times. He also distinguishes miracles from healings, arguing that they are distinct in Scripture:

> That act that makes the lame to go immediately is much different from the laying on of hands, which on a wound being placed, conveys immediately vertue but heals not up under many days or weeks sometimes, according to the quality of the wound. So that wound which by plaister requires long time will also proportionably by that gift take long time, but yet ordinarily cures within half the time the other doth. So that such healings though miraculous, are not in themselves miracles, for that such healings may & usually are effected by physick and by plaister. But yet as to this they are miracles, in that touching the manner and way of cure they are healed without such means, and that by laying on of hands, the form and way in the Apostles' days of conveying the Holy Ghost on believers, and the form and manner always of exercising the gifts of healings proceeding by and from that self same Spirit.[2]

The Baptist leaders in England practised the Biblical injunction of anointing the sick with oil, evidently with a conviction shared by the patient of its curative effect.[3]

---

[1] See Robert Barclay, *Inner Life of the Religious Societies of the Commonwealth* (1876), pp. 218 f., for Dr Gell's Letter to Lady Conway.

[2] *A Whip of Small Cords*, p. 4. Here and elsewhere the modern reader needs to be reminded that 'go' meant walk.

[3] Cf. Adam Taylor, *History of the English General Baptists* (1818), vol. I, p. 452. The custom was based on James v. 14–15. It continued into the eighteenth century in England and America.

Samuel Bownas in his first visit to America noted among the differences between Friends and the 'Quaker Baptists' or followers of John Rogers whom he met in Connecticut 'the anointing of the sick with oil' and adds

Introduction

*The Records of a Church of Christ Meeting at Broadmead,
Bristol 1640–1687* are Baptist accounts parallel in place and
date and even in content to important Quaker sources.
We may note therefore that they contain a circumstantial
narrative of a member who fell distracted in 1673. Physical
means were used to banish his rage, but all in vain. Three
successive days of prayer were held by the church, which
in turn cast out his rage and blasphemy, his horror and
fear, his shame and dumbness, until as the writer concludes,
he 'hath been very well ever since in his body. Magnified
be the Lord!'[1]

A second account referring to twenty years earlier but
recorded after the preceding may be quoted in full:

> One of the members of the congregation, sister Tylly by name,
> had a daughter then about —— years of age, that was bewitched
> as termed; but the child was very much changed and had strange
> fits, and as it were haunted by an evil spirit, that it would say such
> a woman was in the room; though they carried it to Bath. The
> whole church put apart a day for it to seek the Lord by fasting and
> prayer, when brother Jessey was here, and the child was restored
> well as before and to this day. The glory only be given to our
> God.[2]

To other Nonconformists Quakerism itself was a disease
akin to distraction and subject to the curative use of
intercessory prayer. In the Diary of John Angier, pastor
of Denton near Manchester, Lancs, for 14 October 1663,
we read:

> I heard a neighbor was distracted. He had received some books
> from the Quakers and had some acquaintance with them. We

(MS. Journal at Swarthmore College, omitted in printed edition) 'not in use
by any besides themselves that I have heard but never admitted any
unbeliever to be with them in time of prayer over the sick'. For examples of
cures by this means in earlier centuries, see F. W. Puller, *The Anointing of
the Sick in Scripture and Tradition* (2nd ed. 1910).

[1] Edited for the Hanserd Knollys Society by E. B. Underhill (London,
1847), pp. 191–4.

[2] Ibid. pp. 194 f. For other references to Baptist miracles, see below,
pp. 83 f., 95.

prayed with him and it pleased God, though he raged before, and at prayer time, yet after he was very quiet for a time. We besought the Lord for him on the Lord's Day and he was better, blessed be God.[1]

From New England's earliest chronicles, apart from the usual array of 'providences' and 'judgments', few miracles are recorded. John Winthrop has two cases of children's recovery from injury in his Journal under 17 September 1644, a part of his MS. not published until 1825. Both were daughters of members of the Church in Boston, and for both earnest prayers were made by the Church. The cures were evidently recorded as miracles. Winthrop writes:

It may be of use to mention a private matter or two; which fell out about this time, because the power and mercy of the Lord did appear in them in extraordinary manner. One of the deacons of Boston church, Jacob Eliot, (a man of a very sincere heart and an humble frame of spirit,) had a daughter of eight years of age, who being playing with other children about a cart, the hinder end thereof fell upon the child's head, and an iron sticking out of it struck into the child's head and drove a piece of the skull before it into the brain, so as the brains came out, and seven surgeons (some of the country, very experienced men, and others of the ships, which rode in the harbor) being called together for advice, etc., did all conclude, that it was the brains, (being about half a spoonful at one time, and more at other times,) and that there was no hope of the child's life except the piece of skull could be drawn out. But one of the ruling elders of the church, an experienced and very skilful surgeon, liked not to take that course, but applied only plasters to it; and withal earnest prayers were made by the church to the Lord for it, and in six weeks it pleased God that the piece of skull consumed, and so came forth, and the child recovered perfectly; nor did it loose the senses at any time.

Another was a child of one Bumstead, a member of the church, had a child of about the same age, that fell from a gallery in the meeting house about eighteen feet high, and brake the arm and shoulder, (and was also committed to the Lord in the prayers of the church, with earnest desires, that the place where his people

---

[1] *Chetham Society Publications* (1937), N.S. no. 97, p. 130.

assembled to his worship might not be defiled with blood,) and it pleased the Lord that this child was soon perfectly recovered.[1]

EARLY QUAKER MIRACLES

It was natural that the early Friends should expect miraculous power. They testified to the contemporary coming of the Spirit among them in a manner comparable to New Testament times. Visions, insights and prophecies were vouchsafed to them which the event proved to have been true. They recognized Divine providence in their escapes from danger and Divine vengeance in the disasters of their foes. A power to cure could be accepted as no more supernatural than these other recognized phenomena.

While the association of miracles with George Fox was the most conspicuous, other Friends had their experiences. Nayler and his associates in Exeter prison in 1656 believed that he had raised to life a woman that was dead,[2] by laying his hands upon her. Probably she was only in a faint. In any case Nayler made no claim to have raised her by his own power.

The opponents of Quakerism gave circulation to the following account of her own testimony and Nayler's at the time of their arrest in Bristol:

The Examination of James Nayler

Q. How long hast thou lived without any corporal sustenance, having perfect health?

A. Some fifteen or sixteen days, sustained without any other food except the Word of God.

---

[1] *Winthrop's Journal, 'History of New England' 1630–1649* (edited by J. K. Hosmer) in *Original Narratives of Early American History* (1908), vol. II, pp. 209 f. The first girl was Abigail Eliot, niece of the apostle to the Indians. Cotton Mather who gives her first name, mentions also that a silver plate as big as a half-crown was used to close the orifice. He concludes: 'But an history of rare cures in this country would fill more pages than may here be allowed' (*Magnalia Christi Americana*, book VI, ch. II).

[2] This was Dorcas Erbury, daughter of an 'honest minister' in Wales, the well-known William Erbury. See Braithwaite, *Beginnings*, p. 247; Brailsford, *A Quaker from Cromwell's Army*, p. 110. Her Christian name was enough to suggest the story. Cf. Acts ix. 36 ff.

Introduction

Q. Was Dorcas Erbury dead two days in Exeter? And didst thou raise her?

A. I can do nothing of myself: the Scripture beareth witness to the power in me which is everlasting; it is the same power we read of in the Scripture. The Lord hath made me a sign of his coming.

Dorcas Erbury, the Widow of William Erbury, once a Minister, but a seducing Quaker: her Examination

Q. Christ raised those that had been dead; so did not he.

A. He raised me.

Q. In what manner?

A. He laid his hand on my head, after I had been dead two days and said, Dorcas arise: and I arose and live as thou seest.

Q. Where did he this?

A. At the Gaol in Exeter.

Q. What witness hast thou for this?

A. My mother who was present.[1]

It should be recalled that British readers at the time were not unprepared for claims of even the supreme miracle of recovery from death. In 1651, for example, was published at Oxford what purported to be the sober and well-authenticated account by a medical student of the revival of a woman executed by hanging.[2]

A special miraculous intervention is related from Severn, Maryland, in a letter of Robert Clarkson to Elizabeth Harris dated 14th of the 11th month 1657. He says:

Richard Beard was in a miraculous way convinced in the fore part of the summer by a clap of thunder, he being at work in the wood and one more with him in rainy weather. And at that instant it thundered much, as is usual in the summer time, in so much that

---

[1] John Deacon, *The Grand Impostor Examined: or, the Life, Tryal, and Examination of James Nayler* (1656), pp. 18, 33 f.; reprinted 1656 and 1657, and in the *Harleian Miscellany* (1745), vol. vi, pp. 396 f., 399. The work was translated and published in Dutch in 1657. The trial is included in Ralph Farmer, *Sathan Inthron'd in his Chair of Pestilence* (1657), p. 19.

[2] *Newes from the dead, or a true and exact narrative of the miraculous deliverance of Anne Greene, who being executed at Oxford, Decemb. 14, 1650, afterwards revived.*

6

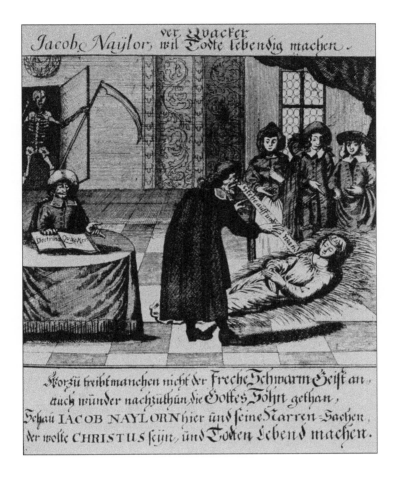

II. James Nayler Raises Dorcas Erbury to Life

it wrought a fear in him and put him to think of his condition. And it did appear to him to be unsafe, he seeing nothing to trust to, there being so many opinions in the world that he did not know which to choose. He then being in fear, not knowing what would become of him in that condition, desired that the Lord would manifest to him concerning the way which was known amongst us whether it was the true way of God or not, and that it might be made known to him by thunder. And at that same instant there came a clap of thunder which was very great in so much that it broke a tree very near them and struck him that was with him to the ground and himself could scarce recover from falling. And a powerful answer came to him at the same instant, that that which he had inquired of was the true way of God; and forthwith he declared it abroad and were (*sic*) convinced thereby wherein I hope he abides.[1]

Miracles of this confirmatory type are rare in the Quaker sources. Sewel supplies a parallel in his account of the converted murderess who was hanged at Bury St Edmunds in 1668. At her execution she prayed for a visible sign that she had been received into God's favour: 'Though it was then a cloudy day, yet immediately after she was turned off, the clouds broke a little and the sun for a few moments shined upon her face, and presently after ceased shining and the sky continued overcast.'[2]

[1] Swarthmore MSS. III, 7, where Robert Clarkson's letter was copied over in one addressed to George Taylor and Thomas Willan by Thomas Hart, dated London, 28th 2nd mo. 1658. This paragraph is omitted by James Bowden, in quoting the letter in his *History of Friends in America*, vol. I, pp. 340 ff. and also by Rufus M. Jones, *Quakers in the American Colonies*, p. 245.

This is probably the Richard Beard who came from Virginia to Maryland, patenting in 1650 a plantation in Anne Arundel County. His home was in South River Hundred next to Severn. He appears frequently in the Maryland records. In 1674 he signed a petition on behalf of the Quakers. He was a member of the Maryland House of Burgesses pretty continuously between 1662 and 1676. By 1681 he had died leaving five children. A few of the facts about him are collected by Hugh B. Johnston, Jr., in *William and Mary College Quarterly* (1938), 2nd ser. vol. XVIII, p. 351.

[2] W. Sewel, *History of the Rise, Increase and Progress of the Christian People Called Quakers* (Philadelphia, 1844), vol. II, p. 160. Her conversion is attributed to William Bennit in this and earlier English editions, but in the original Dutch (1717, p. 547) to John Crook.

Instances of healing are more usual in the Quaker records. An entirely characteristic account is given by John Taylor, later of York, in his Journal, referring to a visit he paid to Nevis in 1662:[1]

I staid about three weeks or more in the island [Nevis], and travelled from meeting to meeting in the town at Haydockes and up in the country. I had one at William Fifield's house, &c. whose only daughter lay very sick at that time; and the doctor, and her parents, with others all looking for her departure.

So I coming to the house, they had me into the room where she lay a dying as they all thought; but I went to the bedside to her, and took her by the hand and stooped down that she might hear me, and asked her, if she had so much faith as to believe she might recover and be raised up to health again? But she was, as it were, speechless, and so weak that she could not speak, they said: yet at length she said, 'yea'. So being then moved of the Lord, I kneeled down by her bedside to prayer in the power of Christ Jesus our Lord; and when I had done I arose up, and presently she arose up and sat upright in her bed, and spake pretty heartily; so that the old doctor and they all, wondered and praised the Lord; the doctor having said before, he had done what he could for her recovery, so would meddle no further but leave her to God's disposing, for he saw no hopes of her recovery.

In the evening I went down to the seaside to the town, in order to go aboard a ship bound for Barbadoes.

But the next morning the young woman got up, and walked out, and took her fowls and made some other provisions, with the help of her mother and father, to send to the ship for my voyage to spend at sea. So by the Lord's power, the young damsel was raised from her sickness to health, to the great admiration of all that knew it.

Another incident on the American continent and perhaps the first to be published in print by Friends as a miracle, though that word is not used, is *A True Discovery and Relation of the Dealings of God with Goodworth Horndall, wife to John Horndall in Newport upon Road-Island in New England*. The seven-page narrative of the mental unrest and recovery of this lady, who because she had once

---

[1] *Memoir of John Taylor* (1710), pp. 17 f.; (1830), pp. 33 f.

relapsed after accepting Quakerism feared she had sinned against the Holy Ghost and was tempted to commit suicide, is described on the main title-page as 'the several late conditions of a Friend upon Road-Iland before, in and after distraction'. The Friend who reassured her and who wrote the narrative was apparently Humphrey Norton, who with John Rous and John Copeland signed as witnesses.[1]

From New England also comes the cryptic account written by Samuel Hooton, son of the early Quaker woman preacher Elizabeth Hooton. 'Something concerning my travel and of the dealings of the Lord with me since the Lord brought me forth from my dwelling' is the title of the MS. preserved in London.[2] The date of the events is not given, apparently they occurred between his mother's last visit in 1664 and her death in 1671. At any rate, Richard Bellingham (d. 1672) was still alive. The place is eastward of Boston, probably about Dover, New Hampshire.

And when I came to the east parts of New England the Lord wrought great things by me there, and many came in amongst us, that the meeting at the eastward way increased much whilst I was with them and the hand of the Lord was with me, praises to his name forever, both in outward miracles and in the work of the Spirit. One woman that had been convinced was nigh unto death that none thought she could have lived, and when the doctor had left her and given her up for dead then was I made glad that so they might see the power of God above the doctor and all outward physicians. So the Lord raised her up by his own power from that very time and she became a fine Friend.

There was another woman that was no Friend that was nigh unto death, and when many people of the world were about her looking when she should depart this life and her husband and family crying I was made to go amongst them to the woman that was nigh death, and when I had kneeled down to pray with her, her spirit revived from that same time, and the Lord healed her and all the people saw it and said it was the Lord's work. And

---

[1] *New England's Ensigne* (1659), pp. 110–16.

[2] Portfolio 3–80 at Friends' Reference Library, printed in *The Friend* (Philadelphia, 1904), vol. LXXVII, pp. 204 ff.

this woman was after a fine and a tender hearted woman, who much loved me, and several that saw it praised God and came to meetings; so that the blessing of God was upon the eastern parts; several great men came; so the word of God was prospered.

The earliest Quaker record of a miracle is perhaps the following in a letter to James Nayler from Richard Farnsworth, dated 'Balbie the 6th of Julie' 1652, and endorsed by Fox himself 'r farworth 1652 a merakell at Chesterfeld':

...the presence of the Lord went along with me, and in Derbyshire at a great market town called Chesterfield, his power was much manifested through me among some of their greatest professors. I was at a stand for hearing them. They have a new gathered church as they call it. But there was one of them that lay under the doctors hand of a fever and I was made instrumental by the Lord, and she was made well.[1]

To Fox himself we are indebted for the following account of a cure by Mary Atkins, a little-known Friend of Dursley Meeting in Gloucestershire:

There was Thomas Atkins and his wife who lived not far off Nailsworth, a shop keeper. And they told me there was a separate meeting of the Presbyterians, and they took an oath of their people that they should neither buy or sell or eat or drink with Friends. And the eminentest woman amongst them fell sick and fell into a benumb condition so as she could neither stir hand or foot, and all the doctors could do her no good.

And at last there came two or three women to Thomas Atkins' wife into her shop, pretending to buy something of her, and she showed them things they asked for, and so they did confess in discourse with her that they had taken an oath as aforesaid, but the occasion of their coming was concerning this woman that lay in that misery, to desire some help and advice from her as to her recovery. And she asked them how they could dispense with their oath and they said they must be forced to break it.

So Thomas Atkins' wife took the woman in hand and cured her. And so the Lord broke the wicked bonds of the Presbyterians

[1] Swarthmore MSS, I, 372.

10

asunder that they had ensnared their people with. And much might be written of these things.[1]

Somewhat later are the instances of recovery narrated of himself by John Richardson (1666–1753) a native of Yorkshire. They were first published in 1757. While he was young he was given to stammering, to the detriment of his preaching, and soon after he was bound apprentice a violent humour fell into one of his legs and caused him much lameness and discouragement about two years. He tells, however, that both ailments were removed when he 'came to believe in Jesus Christ and to press through all to him'.[2] The same kind of cure at request ended his childhood tendency to sore throat, when after a period of petitioning at Hawkshead he says:

I had not been long brought into this devoted and resigned State to be and do what the Lord would have me do, but oh! I felt of the virtue of Christ as a sweet and living Spring by which I was healed.[3]

Not all hopes of success in miracles were fulfilled. John Toldervy, during an interval of 'running out' from Quakerism reports the failure of his first attempt. He was moved to try to bring down fire, as had been done in the days of Moses. He laid a fire of coals and sticks, but when he blew upon it the celestial flame failed to descend and kindle it.[4] Such failures like the failures in prophecy of James Milner and Richard Myers, sometimes mentioned in the same connection, gave a regrettable handle to the opponents of Quakerism.[5]

Such persons were quite as much discredited among

---

[1] II, 152–3. This passage was omitted by Ellwood. The same incident may well have been included in Fox's 'Book of Miracles', but the index does not give any of the probable key words. See, however, no. 67 c.

[2] *An Account of the Life of...John Richardson* (1757), pp. 26, 31 f.

[3] Ibid. p. 57.

[4] John Toldervy, *The Foot out of the Snare* (1656), pp. 30 f. This episode was ridiculed by contemporary and later anti-Quaker writers. See C. Leslie, *The Snake in the Grass* (*Works* (folio, 1721), vol. II, p. 135); John Dove, *An Essay on Inspiration* (1756), p. 7.

[5] I, 107.

Friends because of their failures, as they were among outsiders. Like the two false prophets just mentioned Charles Bayly is described by Fox as one who 'run out'.[1] It is possible that his offence was not unfulfilled prophecy, but unsuccessful efforts at healing. A contemporary unfriendly account says:

> Charles Bayly fell a stroaking, thinking to do some miracles that way, and Richard Anderson fell a cursing—and a certain quaking woman pretended to raise a dead corpse, which when her folly appeared was interred.[2]

Even for well-known Friends the hopes of cure were not always fulfilled. Thus in 1654 Francis Howgill wrote from London with a heavy heart asking Fox's advice:

> Edward Burrough and I were moved to go to a Friend's house in the City who had received the Truth, and her daughter, and a little boy about fifteen years of age being lame of his leg. As I was sitting in the house I looked upon him, and I was struck to the heart and Edward Burrough also not speaking to one the other at all about two hours but waited and our (?) burden was grievous. And the power of the Lord came upon me at last, in great fear and trembling, yet I believed, and was moved to arise up and take the boy by the hand and to say 'In the name and power of God, that raised Jesus from the dead, rise, stand up and walk', and 'If thou believe thou art made whole.' The boy stood up, but as he should have gone, he failed and sat down again. And then Edward Burrough and I was troubled, and yet the Lord doth evidence to me still it was his word. But because of the heathen I am pressed down.[3]

---

[1] II, 5. Apparently it is this Charles Bayly who reappears, after leaving Quakerism, in the unexpected role of the first resident Governor of the Hudson Bay Company in Canada (1670–80). See Grace Lee Nute, *Caesars of the Wilderness* (1943), pp. 131–3.

[2] *Diary of the Rev. John Ward, A.M., Vicar of Stratford-upon-Avon* (edited by Charles Severn, M.D., 1839), p. 287. Stroking was the curative technique of Valentine Greatrakes mentioned below, and others. Richard Anderson figures in the pamphlet war with the Baptists mentioned below. The quaking woman is of course Susanna Pearson.

[3] A. R. Barclay MSS. 21, printed in part in *J.F.H.S.* (1934), vol. XXXI, p. 49. The passage quoted has been heavily crossed out in the original, but its wording is pretty clearly made out. On the back is a long passage in

The 'heathen' made capital out of a more serious failure which occurred not long after and became notorious. Apparently a Friend fell away so far from the truth as to commit suicide, perhaps with the expectation of a miraculous resurrection. A woman Friend promised to raise him from the dead. Neither expectation came true. The man was named William Pool, the woman Susanna Pearson, the date February 1657,[1] the place near Worcester.[2] I quote the account written by Thomas Willan[3] to Margaret Fell. Fox in endorsing it adds the phrase 'mad whimsey':

> There is in the news-book a large matter from Worcester, of a young man that was convinced of the Truth and had some openings, and his mind run out, and so destroyed in the water. And after he was buried his mother made great lamentation, and one Mrs Pearson as they call her, which had been serviceable (it is like) against the priests, and they have gotten something against her. For she told his mother that she would restore her son alive to her. And so she and another woman went to the grave and took him forth, and imitated the prophet, and that not doing went to prayer, and nothing prevailing they buried him again and so the enemy got advantage.[4]

The passage in the 'Newsbook' narrative is readily identified, but has not apparently been noticed by modern Quaker historians. It is well to reprint in full such an early

cipher, not yet decoded. It may contain more information. A careful reproduction was published in *J.F.H.S.* (1905), vol. II, facing p. 1. The system, which seems to combine both phonetic shorthand and arbitrary cipher, is discussed by J. Guthlac Birch, ibid. vol. II, pp. 47–53, who has made some headway with the phonetic signs. The passage is preceded by the appeal: 'Oh my dear brother, one thing hath fallen out this very day that lieth upon my dear brother and me, and in nakedness and in the simplicity of my heart I write to thee that if there be any deceit thou may let me hear a line from [thee] as soon as thou canst.'

[1] Barclay, *Inner Life*, p. 428, says probably 1655; the manuscript cited is endorsed 1654. For full bibliography, see III, 375 f.

[2] Richard Baxter, *Reliquiae Baxterianae* (1696), lib. I, pt. I, § 123, p. 77, says 'at Claines near Worcester'.

[3] A. C. Bickley, *Fox*, pp. 203 f., note, wrongly refers to this letter as written by Thomas Aldam.

[4] Swarthmore MSS. I, 217.

and hostile account for comparison with the partisan Quaker examples to be recounted later:

From Worcester, 28 *February* 1656

Sir, having certain knowledge of the truth of what followes, I thought it my Duty to impart it to your selfe, that the World (especially all good people of this Common-wealth) may by your means receive some further hint of the Palpable seduction and delusion, the apparent Arrogancie, frantick Conceits and Attempts of the Popes English Younglings, the Brood, Sect, and Sort of people called Quakers; the Narrative is of known truth, and will ere long be printed at large, to the open Unmasking of these notorious deceivers and eminently deceived people, here and elsewhere, too too abundantly spread and increased throughout this Land.

One Susan Peirson, having formerly been a pretended Lover of, and a Zealous contender for Christ, Scriptures, Ordinances, Ministers, Members, &c. But all being but (as the end concludes it) meerly pretended, she since hath proved an Appostate from, and been (as I may say) halfe madd against each of the former, and at length she imbarqued among that idle Sect called the Quakers.

Her wonted practice for these late months (Morality, Modesty, and Civility, together with her former pretence of piety, being now laid aside) was this, to wag from one Assembly to another, requiring the Ministers then, and there Preaching, to prove their Call by Miracles, as the Apostles did, and to shew what grounds they had to Preach, by the Book, viz. the Bible; and for their non-performance of the one, and practise of the other, she alledged ordinarily, she was sent by God, and did witness against them, and would often bid them come downe, and forbid them to come and delude the people in such a manner any more; but whether it were to prove her reall call to this practise, or what other end else, I know not; but let the reader judge, and say when all is heard how well she did it.

There was in this City one William Pool an Apprentise to George Knight, (and *qualis est herus talis fuit servus*) both quakers; the young man was aged about 23 years, and on Friday the 20 of February, he went forth of his Masters house about evening into the Garden, and (as tis reported) being asked where he had been, he said he had bin with Christ, Christ had him by the hand, and he had appointed and must be gone again to him.

14

Introduction

But being gone, he came not again, nor was he heard off till
unday following, *February* 22. and then it was found he had
tripped himself, laid his cloaths by the water side, and drowned
imself, and accordingly by the Coroner and his quest was judged
uilty of self-murther, and was buried in the Parish of *Clains*, by
our of the clock on Monday morning, his Mother, an honest and
y report of some judicious people that know her) a godly woman,
eing much troubled hereat, the aforesaid Mistress *Peirson*
ndeavored to comfort her with this perswasion, That she would
tch her son to her alive again; and about six or seven hours after
e was buried, the said Mistress *Peirson* and other Quakers went
o the grave, digged up the yong man, opened the shroud and laid
he Corps upon the ground, rubbed his face and brest with her hand
and some say, laid her face upon his face, and her hands upon his
ands) and commanded him to rise. But he not moving, she
neeled down and prayed over him, and so commanded him in the
ame of the living God, to arise and walk. This being done, and he
ot obeying, she caused him to be put into the Grave again, and
hence departed, having onely this excuse left her, *That he had not
et been dead four days.* Since this we have enjoyed one Lecture
ays Sermon without her disturbance; she like the Snail, pulling
her Horns. And I hope, that by these and such like eminent
etections, it will be known, by what spirit it is, that they are
uided, and how they deceive and are deceived.[1]

*This will be at-
tested by many
Witnesses of
known credit.*

Another story of earlier date but similar in its self-
estructive traits Fox endorsed 'a merekell'. It is reported
o Margaret Fell by James Nayler, apparently in mid-April,
654, but without place or date:

The priests in these parts are exceeding mad and cruel. They have
ad great meetings to plot what to do but everything is ordered to
heir torment. One of them hath a son and two daughters convinced
f the truth, and he sent and got twelve more priests to come to
urn them, but they stand steadfast, and the young man was made
ery bold. One priest struck off his hat, another bade send him to
Iouse of Correction, another bade slit his skin from his back to his
et, other bade bind him and whip him, and all went away in

---

[1] *Mercurius Politicus*, 26 February to 5 March, 1657, no. 351, pp. 7639 f.
nd *The Publick Intelligencer*, March 2 to March 9, 1657, pp. 1234 f. For
usanna Pearson, see III, 375. She and George Knight continued to be
uakers. See Joseph Besse, *Sufferings*, Index, under 'Worcestershire'.

great rage. But since a temptation hath befallen the young man which hath set them all on fire. About midnight he had a voice which said, 'Up, get thee hence.' And he did arise and went forth, but the mind not waiting to be guided but running before he lost his guide and so returned home again. And the tempter got in and tempted him strongly to destroy himself bidding him cast himself into the fire, persuading him he should not burn. But at length he grew so high that he prevailed with him to put his hand into a kettle full of boiling liquor that was on the fire, and they report that he held it in a quarter of an hour. This was done in a great town and a wicked one.... The young man is well recovered out of the temptation and his hand recovers very fast, which is praises to our God and a mighty wonder.[1]

The cases just recounted were extreme. More characteristic were the recoveries from illness like that described of Richard Davies by his daughter, Tace Endon. In December 1688, nineteen years before his death, Davies was at his home in Welshpool 'very sick and very weak, so that most that saw him, thought he would not recover'. But two visiting ministers, Robert Barrow and Robert Haydock, coming into those parts held a meeting at Davies' house, prayed for his recovery and finally Barrow predicted that they would see each at the following Yearly Meeting in London, which they did.[2]

Mariabella Farmborough (1626–1708) was believed to have been miraculously cured of lameness very late in a long life. Her son-in-law, Peter Briggins, wrote of her:

Though in her old age (by the hardships she met with in prisons) she was afflicted with lameness by reason whereof she used pretty much to be confined at home, yet she would go as often as possible her health would let her (and indeed I have thought beyond her natural strength) she pretty constantly attended the women's meeting that takes care of the poor and was one of our most serviceablest. And she with Mary Elson used to go and visit the sick &c. and to meetings, though it was with crutches. Yet it

---

[1] Swarthmore MSS. III, 192. The words beginning 'since a temptation' and ending 'a wicked one' have been crossed through.

[2] *An Account of Richard Davies*, unpaged prefatory 'testimony concerning my dear and loving father Richard Davies', 1710, and subsequent editions.

pleased the Lord miraculously to give her strength though near 80 years of age, anew, so that she walked without her crutches to meetings &c., until her last illness.[1]

Granted the easy belief in miracles, passages that we should not so classify may have been so intended by the writers. William Edmondson of Ireland writes of a journey in 1676 or 1677 in the Indian-infested country between Virginia and Carolina of a recovery of this sort:

We took our journey through the wilderness and in two days came well to Carolina first to James Hall's house who went from Ireland to Virginia with his family. His wife died there, and he had married the widow Phillips at Carolina and lived there; but he had not heard that I was in those parts of the world. When I came into the house, I saw only a woman servant; I asked for her master, she said he was sick. I asked for her mistress, she said she was gone abroad. I bid her show me into the room wher[e] her master lay; so I went into the room, where he was laid on the bed, sick of an ague with his face to the wall. I called him by his name, and said no more; he turned himself and looked earnestly at me a pretty time, and was amazed; at last he asked if that was William? I said yes. He said he was affrighted, for he thought it had been my spirit; so he presently got up, and the ague left him, and did not return. He travelled with me the next day, and kept me company whilst I staid in that part.[2]

Providences and coincidences are reported by Friends, hardly distinguishable in their own sight, from miracles and examples. Thus Besse records of some persecuted Friends on the Isle of Man in September 1659:

One morning, as soon as they came on shore, having been all night in the wet and cold at sea (for they were fishermen), they were

---

[1] *Eliot Papers* (1894), vol. II, pp. 3 f. Her husband was Thomas Farmborough of St Paul's Churchyard, London. In spite of the clear difference in spelling her name it is she and her lameness that are mentioned by Mary Lower in a letter to her mother, Margaret Fox, 2, 3rd mo., 1701: 'Marabellon Thombora (*sic*) desires to be remembered to thee. She is my next neighbor and hath been lamely in her foot. The fever fell into it and she hath kept her chamber I think above half a year.' (Thirnbeck MSS. 28, printed in *J.F.H.S.* (1912), vol. IX, p. 185; L. V. Hodgkin, *A Quaker Saint of Cornwall*, pp. 214 f.)

[2] *Journal of the Life of William Edmondson* (1715), p. 99. With the last sentence compare the endings of nos. 16 *a*, 21 *a* and 75 *b*.

hurried to prison in their wet clothes and detained several days in the midst of their herring-fishery, the most advantageous season for their business; though they lost not thereby, for the night next after they were released they caught as many fish as they were able to bring on shore, so that they could not but gratefully acknowledge a peculiar hand of Providence attending them.[1]

In the use of the term miracle the early Friends were not thinking of any carefully defined distinction. Scarcely anyone in that day would have offered a definition such as modern science suggests. A theological distinction between miracles and providences was in some quarters of great importance. This is shown in the trial of Anne Hutchinson before the General Court of Massachusetts Bay Colony, meeting at Newtown, now Cambridge, in November 1637. Her accusers were of course prepared to find fault with all her claims of special revelation and miraculous action, but by an illogical distinction they accepted portents and special providences. She herself evidently shared the distinction, or at least recognized the trap, for when asked whether she expected to be delivered by miracle as Daniel was, she replied: 'I look that the Lord should deliver me by his providence.' The Rev. John Cotton, of Boston, observed that as to miracles he was not sure that he understood her; but, he added: 'If she doth expect a deliverance in a way of Providence, then I cannot deny it....If it be by way of miracle, then I would suspect it.' He was kind enough to believe the accused shared this distinction.[2]

The term providences continued to be an acceptable one in New England theology and popular thought and so indeed elsewhere, so that a recent study finds something unusual and almost akin to modern science in the restraint with which the colonial historian, William Hubbard, employs the term.[3] Although early Friends sometimes

---

[1] Joseph Besse, *An Abstract of the Sufferings*, etc., 1733, vol. I, p. 127. The influence of the Gospel accounts of a miraculous draft of fishes is obvious.

[2] Charles Francis Adams, *Three Episodes of Massachusetts History* (1892), pp. 502–4.

[3] Kenneth B. Murdock, 'William Hubbard and the Providential Interpretation of History' in *Proc. Amer. Antiq. Soc.* (1943), vol. LII, pp. 15–37.

used Providence in the singular, as in that striking Journal of Jonathan Dickinson, *God's Protecting Providence, Man's Surest Help and Defence*, etc. (1699), the word seems to have been infrequent in the plural. Instead where other writers would have said providences, they let the story point its own moral or used without theological or scientific inhibition the simple biblical term miracle. They were no more keen than were their contemporaries to vindicate themselves by evidence of Divine approval shown in remarkable escapes, especially in travel, that were vouchsafed their own members, or in the horrible disasters that befell their enemies. The underlying philosophy behind their 'Judgments' and 'Examples' and behind their less systematic but frequent record of escapes was the same as in their accounts of cures. That philosophy was also shared under different terminology by their contemporaries, both religious and superstitious.

QUAKER MIRACLES BOTH RIDICULED AND DEMANDED

The Quaker claim of miracles was familiar to their opponents, and not only in cases where the latter could taunt them with failure. Writing from Leith in Scotland on 22 June 1658, Timothy Langley informed Secretary Thurloe:

For present all that I discern is that the Quakers are altogether retrograde, though now some of them pretend miracles.[1]

In the preamble to the act against the Quakers passed in Virginia in March 1660, they are described as

an unreasonable and turbulent sort of people, commonly called Quakers, who contrary to law do daily gather together unto them unlawful assemblies and congregations of people, teaching and publishing lies, miracles, false visions, prophecies and doctrines,

---

[1] *Thurloe State Papers*, vol. VII, p. 194. Printed also in *J.F.H.S.* (1911), vol. VIII, p. 165.

2-2

which have influence upon the communities of men both ecclesiastical and civil, etc.[1]

In 1660 Richard Blome ridicules the claim of a Quaker 'that when the fulness of time was come he should work miracles'.[2]

In the same volume is narrated the discomfiture of a Quaker who expected James Parnell to be raised from the dead after his fast and death in Colchester. Thomas Underhill, from whom the story is probably derived, gives the matter in more detail:

> And after he was laid in his grave, a man Quaker (how many more than one I cannot say) waited by his grave until the end of three days, expecting his resurrection, but James not rising, the poor man ran mad upon it, and so continued many weeks, but at last got loose both from his madness and Quaking, through God's mercy to him.[3]

This is for Underhill only one illustration of his thesis that the Quakers 'do exceedingly covet that which they say they have but have not, namely the gift of working miracles'. A few pages earlier he ridicules the answer of the Friends Fox and Hubberthorne to the reply of Gabriel Camelford, parson of Staveley Chapel, to one of the queries set him by Thomas Atkinson, of Cartmel, in 1652. The Quakers assert what their opponents on their part deny of

---

[1] Hening, *Statutes at Large of Virginia*, vol. I, p. 532, quoted in Weeks, *Southern Quakers and Slavery*, p. 16. One wonders whether the 'miracles' included the incident of Robert Beard cited above.

[2] *The Fanatick History* (1660), p. 137. James Nayler, *A Short Answer to a Book called the Fanatick History* (1660), pp. 12 f., replies curtly that Nicholas Kate, the man so charged, was not known by the Quakers, and the accusation against him is therefore not their concern.

[3] *Hell Broke Loose* (1660), p. 36. To this as to several other of the charges against the Quakers in this literature wide circulation was given by its inclusion in successive editions of Samuel Clarke's *A Mirrour, or Looking-Glasse for Saints and Sinners*. The story can be traced back to 11 April 1656, the day after his death, when the vicar of the neighbouring Earls Colne wrote so in his Diary. Three days later he added: 'Its said in the country that his party went to Colchester to see his resurrection again.' *The Diary of the Rev. Ralph Josselin, 1616–1683*, ed. by E. Hockliffe (*Royal Historical Society Publications*. Camden, 3rd ser. (1908), vol. xv).

them: 'The same gift that was in the Apostles we witness, the blind see, the deaf hear, the lame walk and them that have laid long under such false physicians as thou art are cured.'[1]

Ralph Farmer, another anti-Quaker writer of the same period scoffs at the idea of Quaker miracles. He explains their claims in different ways:

These wretches work no Miracles for as for making Proselytes and procuring Followers (which are all the Miracles they usually pretend to) beside that this cannot be a miracle I say beside that Deceivers and Impostors in all ages have done such.[2]

A merchant of this City [Bristol] upon the Road discoursing with one of them, and demanding of him what miracles they wrought to justifie their extraordinary call; he answered, We do work miracles but thou hast no eyes to see them.[3]

It is worth noting that the earliest printed reference to a reputed miracle of Fox or indeed of any Friend comes from anti-Quaker sources which mention the attempted but unsuccessful cure of a lame man near Kendal. The date is probably as early as 1652, for in the following year Francis Higginson published the following allusion:

It was a strange bold piece of Impiety in George Fox in commanding a Criple at a place near Kendal to throw away his crutches, as though he had been invested with a power to work Miracles, but the Criple remained a Criple still, and George Fox impudently discovered his own folly.[4]

The earliest report of a group of Quaker miracles also comes from a hostile source. Writing in 1656, Jonathan

---

[1] Underhill, op. cit. p. 17, referring to George Fox and Richard Hubberthorne, *Truth's Defence against the Refined Subtlety of the Serpent* (York, 1653), pp. 43 f.

[2] *Sathan Inthron'd in his Chair of Pestilence* (1657), p. 52.

[3] *The Great Mysteries of Godlinesse and Ungodlinesse* (1655), p. 87. To this specific charge the Quaker reply by John Audland, *The Innocent Delivered out of the Snare* (1655), makes no reference.

[4] *A Brief Relation of the Irreligion of the Northern Quakers* (1653), p. 29. The incident is related in much the same way in John Deacon, *An Exact History of the Life of James Naylor* (1657), pp. 49 f., derived from the earlier passage which is specifically cited.

Clapham, the minister at Wramplingham in Norfolk, in a chapter entitled 'The Quakers Pretend to Miracles' relates, he says, 'a few of those pretended miracles, that I have had from some of them reported to myself'.

One of them (now or lately in prison at Bury) being called to the Ministry (say they) and questioning at first, whether his call was from God, desired a signe for the confirmation thereof, that by touching or speaking to a woman, who then lay very sick, she might be recovered and restored to health, which doing (saith the reporter) she immediately recovered. Another of them being put into a dungeon and there kept for some days without any meat, became very hungry, whereupon he was bidden by the voice within him to arise and eat, and was directed to a place neer the grate, where were many ugly spiders, of which he took and did eate till he was satisfied thereby as well as if he had eaten of the wholesomest food in the world. Two others of them being in prison at Chester (or some other place in the West, for the reporter could not certainly tell me what place) were singing Psalmes together, a thing they so highly exclaime against others for doing, and suddenly such a glorious light shone into the prison as made the Jaylor come trembling, and fall down before them, whereupon he and his houshold were converted to them that day.[1] One in the North, (as it was confidently reported to me by themselves) did fast full fourty dayes and fourty nights together without taking any food. The wife of Coll. Benson[2] (saith the same reporter) being with child went to York upon some message from God to oppose the Priests, where not being known, she was cast into Prison, and

---

[1] What is evidently this very event is related by a participant, Thomas Holme, in a letter from Chester, 5 April 1654 (Swarthmore MSS. I, 190).

[2] The imprisonment at York in 1653 of Dorothy, wife of Gervase Benson, of Sedbergh is mentioned in the Quaker records (Besse, *Suff.*, vol. II, p. 80; *F.P.T.* p. 251 n.), also her son's name Immanuel born in prison 2 February 1653/4. But of her anticipated painless delivery—a feature probably derived from the miracles of Jesus' birth in the apocryphal gospels—Friends make no mention, though we have a letter from her husband to George Fox telling of her state: 'Ann Blaykling I left with her....It was of the Lord Ann Blaykling's coming to York, my wife expecting every hour since she got thither to fall into travail. Praises to him forever.' (Swarthmore MSS. IV, 33; Sedbergh, 23 December 1653.) More miraculous expectations of the birth of a child are attributed to George and Margaret Fox (see *P.M.H.B.* (1946), vol. LXX, p. 354 and note), to John Robins the Ranter and his wife (see *D.N.B.* s.v.) and Joanna Southcott (*D.N.B.* s.v.).

delivered of a childe there, but before her delivery told those with her, that she should feel no paine in her travel, and should have a man-childe, whose name should be Immanuel, which child was shewed afterward to the Protector for a wonder. Many aged and infirme women (say they) since they came into this way, out of weaknesse have become strong and able to travel hundreds of miles on foot.

These things being objected against by me, as being done far off, and most of them in corners, and therefore far unlike the miracles done by Christ and the Apostles, I desired to hear of some done neerer hand, the truth of which I might finde out; whereupon I was informed of one in this Town wherein I live and another at Norwich. That in this Town was reported to me (as neer as I can remember) in these very words. Was it not a Miracle for T.C. that had been brought so low by a Quartane Ague to be so suddenly recovered? I answered it was a merciful providence, but not miracle; and further demanded by what means he was cured? It was replyed, that Richard Hubberthorne, did but go to his door and speak to him, and presently he recovered; but afterwards enquiring of the man himself, what Hubberthorne said to him, he told me, he said nothing, but bade him look to the light in him, he did not rebuke his distemper, nor command him in the name of Christ to arise and walk; and since that time this man hath continued in a languishing condition.

That other pretended miracle at Norwich, was upon Thomas Symonds Weaver,[1] one of their speakers, a letter whereof I read, subscribed with his own hand. It was this, that upon a Lords day (some few moneths agon) the hand of the Lord was upon him from morning to evening very sore; and he was smitten with a tormenting pain in his bowels, and nothing that his friends about him applied

---

[1] Thomas Symonds was converted to Quakerism at Stourbridge Fair, Cambridge, in 1654, before Richard Hubberthorne and George Whitehead came to Norwich later the same year (*J.F.H.S.* (1921), vol. xviii, pp. 22 f.). The latter says in his later autobiography: 'The most noted serviceable Friend in that City was Thomas Symonds, a Master Weaver, who received Travelling Friends; he was a loving honest man, and came to receive a gift in the ministry and was faithful unto death' (*Christian Progress* (1725), p. 24). The first Quaker meetings at Norwich were held in his house. Later he moved to Pulham in Norfolk where he died 23 September 1666. See A. J. Eddington, *The First Fifty Years of Quakerism in Norwich* (1932), pp. 6, 7, 22, 272. Symonds' supposed letter about his recovery does not appear to survive either in manuscript or in print.

could help him, insomuch that they gave him over as irrecoverable, whereupon the voice within him bade him take a draught of cold water, which he doing in the obedience of faith, his spirits revived, and himself presently recovered, and sent out a letter of this to his friends that they might give glory for it to-God, and be thereby further confirmed and established in their way.[1]

Two years earlier Ephraim Pagitt, adding to his *Heresiographie* sections on the Quakers and the Ranters, says of the former: 'In their private Conventicles they pretend to acting of Miracles, as turning water into wine, dispossessing of Divels, &c.'[2]

Beside their repudiation of Quaker miracles, the opponents of Quakerism demanded miracles as credentials. There were for example the Seekers. We learn from many sources of their demand for miracles. Richard Baxter writes of them: 'These taught that our Scripture was uncertain; that present miracles are necessary to faith, that our ministry is null and without authority, etc.'[3] John Crook the Quaker says that they 'denied that there was visibly to be found either true church or ministry in England that they knew of, rightly constituted for want of an administrator, qualified with gifts and manifesting their sending by miracles'.[4] It was certainly partly for this reason that many of the Seekers remained aloof from Quakerism as they did from all organized religion. But as Crook himself admits, there were also a different sort.

---

[1] Jonathan Clapham, *A Full Discovery and Confutation of the wicked and damnable Doctrines of the Quakers* (1656), pp. 44–6. The answers to this book by Richard Hubberthorne, *Truth and Innocencie Clearing Itself and its Children* (1657), and by George Fox, *The Great Mistery of the Great Whore Unfolded* (1659), make no mention of this particular passage.

[2] 'Fift [*sic*] edition' (1654), p. 140.

[3] *Reliquiae Baxterianae* (1696), lib. I, pt. I, § 121, p. 76.

[4] *A Short History of the Life of John Crook* (1706), Introduction (page unnumbered); reprinted in *Friends' Library* (Philadelphia (1849), vol. XIII, p. 205). According to an earlier writer in a pamphlet called *A Relation of Severall Heresies* (1646), p. 15, they claimed that 'it is the will of God that miracles should attend the ministry as in primitive times' (cited in Barclay, op. cit. p. 176 n.). Further evidence of this expectation in Seeker circles is given by R. M. Jones in *Studies in Mystical Religion*, pp. 454, 456, 458. See also his foreword to this volume.

Saltmarsh, for example, anticipated the Quaker principle of belief in truth through direct revelation and without miracle. He says:

> If there must be miracles (as some hold in order to insure belief) then Truth is not of that excellent nature that it seems.... If there must be miracles to make us believe and not believe any Truth till then, we must have for every truth as well as for one or two a miracle to give it evidence and so there must be a continual and new miracle working for every believer.... No miracles can in their own nature make one believe without a spiritual conviction from the Spirit of Christ going along with it.[1]

Probably we should class among the Seekers that Clement Writer who is known to us from many sources. We read that in 1656 at the house of Sarah Drews in Worcester there was 'a dispute with one Clement Writer, who would have George Fox and Friends confirm their doctrine by miracles'.[2] Thomas Edwards in his *Gangraena*[3] describes one 'Clement Wrighter' in London as 'an arch-heretic and fearful apostate' who 'said that there is no Gospel, no ministry nor no faith, nor can be unless any can show as immediate a call to the ministry as the Apostles had, and can do the same miracles as they did'. Richard Baxter who was a near neighbour also refers to Clement Writer. In fact the two men carried on a literary warfare, which included two pamphlets of Writer, now rare, and Baxter's *Unreasonableness of Infidelity*. The latter describes 'those apostates in England who go under the name of Scepticks or Seekers' as maintaining 'that Miracles being ceased, there are now no churches, Christians, ministers or scriptures known to them, and that the world for want of such miracles is not now bound to believe the Gospel'.[4] Of Writer himself Baxter says

---

[1] *Smoak in the Temple*, p. 20, quoted by R. M. Jones, *Mysticism and Democracy in the English Commonwealth*, p. 94.

[2] *F.P.T.* p. 276. Fox's letter to Writer referring to this interview is in Swarthmore MSS. VII, 16; cf. Braithwaite, *Beginnings of Quakerism*, p. 202. On Clement Writer, see *D.N.B.* s.v.

[3] (1646), pt. I, § 2, p. 27.

[4] *Unreasonableness of Infidelity* (1655), pt. I (second pagination), pp. 1 ff.

that he 'had long seemed a forward professor of religiousness and of a good conversation, but was now perverted to I know not what. A Seeker he professed to be, but I easily perceived that he was either a juggling Papist or an infidel.... His assertion to me was that no man is bound to believe in Christ that doth not see confirming miracles himself with his own eyes'.[1] More conventional men held the same views.[2]

The view of many others than Baptists is probably expressed in the distinction made by Thomas Grantham:

> Though we hold it unsafe to say miraculous gifts are so ceased, as that the Church may in no case ask them, yet we say, if men should show signs to prove themselves apostles it would now rather prove them deceivers.[3]

The demand for miracles was made of the Quakers by the more orthodox groups in both written and oral argument, and was regularly refused by them. For the former may be cited Samuel Eaton, an Independent teacher in Cheshire who in 1654 declared: 'All that pray by the spirit and speak by the spirit and do not show a miracle are impostors.'[4] In an anonymous but immediate reply the Quakers answered: 'And wonders and miracles and signs are amongst them [the Quakers] but your adulterous generation could never believe.'[5] George Fox himself made answer to the same book five years later. On this point his answer also is very brief. He says: 'Many prayed by the spirit and spake by the spirit, that did not show miracles at the tempter's command, though among

---

[1] *Reliquiae Baxterianae* (1696), lib. I, pt. I, § 182, p. 116.

Baxter elsewhere, though quoting with approval the view of Humfredus: 'There is now no need of miracles, the word having sounded forth into the whole earth,' admits contemporary providences and cures in answer to prayer, including in his own case the cure of a tumour on the tonsil. (*Saints' Everlasting Rest*, pt. II, ch. VI, §§ III–VI.)

[2] See the quotation from Edward Stillingfleet in Barclay, op. cit. pp. 211 f.

[3] *Christianismus Primitivus, or the Ancient Christian Religion* (1678), bk. IV, p. 163.

[4] *The Quakers Confuted* (1654), p. 14. On Eaton see *D.N.B.*

[5] *An Answer to a Book which Samuel Eaton put up to Parliament* (1654), p. 16.

believers there are miracles in the spirit which are signs and wonders to the world as Isaiah saith.'[1]

Whether Fox means literal miracles performed by the spirit or spiritual or mystical miracles such as Friends elsewhere seem to appeal to as curing those spiritually blind, etc., or raising the dead mystically,[2] is not clear. The phrase is later regarded as characteristic of the Quaker. John Faldo replying to William Penn in 1675 says: 'Some-newcoyn'd phrases you use which are your proper and peculiar mintage (except you had them from Jacob Behem) *ex. gr.* Miracles in Spirit, The Seed in Captivity, A measure of God,' etc.[3]

As for oral debates on the subject similar to that between Fox and Writer in 1656, we may add one between James Nayler and certain Baptists in 1656,[4] and the experience of George Whitehead, who, when in 1655 at the house of Lady Hubbard at Norwich he declared that he had a measure of the same Spirit, as Christ and the apostles had, though in less degree of attainment, was challenged by the Lady's chaplain to prove it by some sign or miracle as the apostles did.[5]

On the Continent, as in England, the opponents of Quakerism would expect Friends to justify any claim to direct inspiration by producing the credential of miracles. John Hall, reporting on visits he paid in 1657 to 'steeple houses' in Copenhagen in Denmark, tells of a 'priest that asked him whether his call was mediate or immediate. If mediate (saith he), by whom? If immediate where was his miracles? But because John answered him not according to his will, therefore fell he into a rage'.[6]

---

[1] *The Great Mistery of the Great Whore* (1659), p. 3 (*Works* (1831), vol. III, p. 37).

[2] See below p. 63 note.

[3] John Faldo, *XXI Divines (whose Names are here-under affixed) Cleared, of the Unjust Criminations of Will Penn*, p. 25.

[4] Swarthmore MSS. III, 76, a letter from Nayler to Fox. Though endorsed 1654 it probably belongs April-May 1656.

[5] *The Christian Progress of George Whitehead* (1725), pp. 55 f.

[6] Letter of William Caton to Margaret Fell, Amsterdam, 15 November 1657 (Caton MSS. III, 39).

An account is preserved by Willem Sewel of the discussion with Galenus Abrahamsz at Amsterdam held by the Quaker delegation to the Continent in October 1677.[1] The Mennonite leader, like the Seekers above mentioned, maintained 'That no one now-a-days could be accepted as a messenger of God, unless he confirmed his teaching by miracles.' 'Penn', continues the historian, 'did not want for arguments to oppose to this assertion, since the Christian religion had been once already confirmed by miracles, and therefore such things were now needless among Christians.'[2]

Barclay is not mentioned on that occasion, but shortly before he had dealt with the question in a correspondence with a notable Hollander, Adriaan Paets, ambassador of the States-General to Spain, and later commissioner for the Dutch East India Company. Writing to Christian Hartzoeker about the doctrine of the Quakers, Paets had declared that

Men are not even obliged to believe God producing any revelation in the soul concerning matter of fact, whether of a thing done or to be done, unless there be added some miracles obvious to the outward senses, by which the soul may be ascertained, that that revelation cometh from God.

Barclay's reply, originally in Latin, is based on the Scripture evidence that John the Baptist did no miracle,

---

[1] On Galenus Abrahamsz de Haan, see C. B. Hylkema's short biography as well as his accounts in *Mennonitisches Lexikon*, vol. II, p. 28, and in his *Reformateurs*, passim. Penn expected to prepare an account of the debate as shown by his letters to the Countess of Hoorn from Brill (*Journal*, p. 274) and to Pieter Hendricks from London (9th mo. 19, 1674; *B.F.H.A.* (1911), vol. IX, p. 6). The MS. of his continental journal, in the hand of Mark Swanner, now in the possession of the Historical Society of Pennsylvania, gives a heading: 'A Brief Relation of the most substantial passages in two conferences held at Amsterdam between Galenus Abrahamus and William Penn in the presence of a free and large auditory', but it is followed by a blank. Fox gives little information about the debate, Croese gives less. See W. I. Hull, *William Penn and the Dutch Quaker Migration to Pennsylvania*, 1935, pp. 85–92.

[2] Hull, op. cit. p. 91. Cf. Sewel, *History* (Philadelphia (1844), vol. II, pp. 259 ff.). Much of the following matter is probably Sewel's argument rather than part of the historic debate.

and many prophets prophesied and did no miracle. Truth was revealed in dreams without miracle. Fallible as is the inner sense, the outward sense is fallible too, as the experience of false miracles testifies.[1]

More briefly but along the same lines Barclay had dealt with the subject in his well-known *Apology*:[2]

> We need not miracles because we preach no new gospel, but that which is already confirmed by all the miracles of Christ and his apostles...which we are ready and able to confirm by the testimony of the scriptures. This is the common Protestant answer [to the Papists], therefore may suffice in this place.

George Keith, who accompanied Penn, Fox and Barclay in 1677 to the Continent had also recently expressed himself on the relation of miracles to direct revelation. In his *Immediate Revelation not Ceased* he says:

> We do not hereby understand any of these ways following as of necessary continuance. 1. Not any outward audible voice, framed by the Lord immediately in the air, and presented by the outward ear. 2. Nor any outward visible appearance presented to the outward eye, neither by the ministry of angels, nor by the ministry of Christ, in the outward. 3. Nor dreams and visions upon the imagination in the night season, nor yet by trances so called, which is by a cessation of the exercise of all the outward senses. 4. Nor any outward miracles....So that all these ways of God's appearing and revealing himself, in, by or under outward appearances; or in dreams or night visions, were but very shadowy and remote, and rather mediate than immediate: this alone appearance and revelation of God in his own Seed and birth in man, is the most near, and most immediate; and giveth unto man the most intuitive and clear and open and satisfactory knowledge of God, that he is capable of in his highest supernatural elevation.[3]

Penn had expressed himself on the subject in 1671, replying in collaboration with George Whitehead to an

---

[1] Sewel, op. cit. vol. II, pp. 232, 234, 243.
[2] First printed in Latin 1676, in English 1678. See Proposition X, § XII.
[3] George Keith, *Immediate Revelation* (1676), pp. 7, 17, cited by Rachel Hadley King in her MS. thesis *George Fox and the Light Within, 1650–1660* (1937), p. 104, but not included in the essay as published under the same title (Philadelphia, 1940). This work was written by Keith in 1665 and the first edition of 1668 contains these passages on pp. 4, 11.

attack on Quakerism by Thomas Jenner. Denying not the fact of miracles, but their necessity Penn said:

> That the only sign and evidence of inspiration is miracles I utterly renounce and deny as what is most false and unworthy of the reason, perspicuity, and self evidencing verity of the Christian religion.

> I need not go far to detect the falsity of the assertion, since many, nay most of the prophets are not recorded to have worked any. And if the Scriptures are acknowledged to have been given forth by the Holy Ghost, how many mentioned in them, whose words and works compile them, never worked so much as one miracle, and that both under the Old and New Testament?...

> But how weak an argument the doctrine of miracles is to prove the verity of the Christian faith or revelation at this time of day is best seen by considering it was weakness that occasioned them.... We have received and maintained our faith in Christ by more noble and sublime arguments than that of miracles, namely the truth, reason, equity, holiness and recompense of the Christian religion, which miracles can never render more or less intrinsically so.

> Not that we put a low esteem upon miracles, but comparatively only. And to say they are ceast is in no other sense true, than that wherein vision or revelation is: I mean they are ceast to them that have not faith. For many have and do know the power of taking up their sick beds and walk; and whose faith in God's power has made them whole.[1]

The discussion on miracles in 1677 of these English visitors in Holland is all the more interesting in the light of two nearly contemporary episodes connected with Dutch Quakerism, both of which have left a printed record. One was the cure, to be mentioned later, of Jeske Claes after fourteen years of inability to walk. This had occurred in 1676 and was noted by Friends as a genuine miracle.[2] The other was the claim of an Amsterdam Friend, in fact the very Friend at whose house the debate with Galenus Abrahamsz occurred, one Cornelis Roelofs, to

[1] *A Serious Apology for the Principles and Practices of the People Called Quakers* (1671), pt. II, pp. 86–8 (reprinted in *A Collection of the Works of William Penn* (1726), vol. II, pp. 38–9).

[2] See below, pp. 61–2.

have worked or to expect to work a cure upon a man long insane at the town of Franeker. On 28th of 4 mo. 1678, immediately upon his return from Friesland, seven of the Amsterdam Friends interviewed Roelofs and declared to him that his pretended prophecies, miracles and wonders were only false imaginings, and wrote an account disclaiming the responsibility of Quakerism for them. Their testimony with an endorsement by the Quarterly Meeting was published in pamphlet form, to clear the Society from the stigma of such unfounded supernatural pretensions.[1]

In his important discussion of Fox's miraculous cures Neave Brayshaw cites (with references not here repeated) other evidence of Friends' negative view towards miracles:

Mary Penington says that before she professed with Friends (in 1658) she 'had heard objected against them that they wrought not miracles'....Dr George Hickes, preaching before the University of Oxford in 1680, said that anyone who professed to know this spiritual experience ought to exercise these powers. Isaac Penington, in reply to these demands on Quakerism, did not bring up in evidence the cures wrought by Fox or by any other Friend, but asserted that miracles were no longer necessary (they 'leave a dispute in the mind' he says); and that if anyone did work them, they would furnish no evidence of the source whence they came except to the eye that would already see.[2]

The early Quaker view of miracles is well summed up by Edward Smith in his *Life of William Dewsbury*. Neither Fox,

his companions, nor his successors in belief, have ever laid great stress on such occurrences however true; and have avoided

---

[1] *Getuygenis tegens Cornelis Roelofsz. van der Werff (van de Vergad. der Vrienden [Kwakers] te Amsterdam, over door hem geveinsde mirakelen...)*, Rotterdam, 1678. A full account of the episode was to have been included in W. I. Hull's later monographs on Dutch Quaker history. See his *William Penn and the Dutch Quaker Migration to Pennsylvania*, 1935, p. 240, n. 308.

[2] *The Personality of George Fox* (1933), pp. 173 f. With the citation from Mary Penington compare the words of her husband, Isaac Penington: 'It is likewise excepted against us that we do not work miracles', quoted by F. S. Turner, *The Quakers* (1889), p. 119.

insisting upon them as proof of their ministry. And although Friends did...acknowledge such instances of the marvellous extension of divine regard to be consistent with Scripture and sound reason, they concluded it to be proper in these latter ages of the church to receive them simply as collateral assurances, that the Lord's power is the same in one day as another, rather than as essential evidences or as requisite fruits of true faith.[1]

QUAKER CLAIMS AND CAUTION

While the Friends generally refused miracles asked of them, they did not hesitate to stake their own claims on miracles, and to urge their opponents to such a test. Perhaps fasting does not seem to us quite as miraculous now as it did to the early Friends, and we read in Fox's *Journal* of various fasts by him and by others lasting several days. Evidently the survival in such cases was regarded by the Friends as a miracle,[2] while their opponents eagerly seized upon the idea that some of them had killed themselves by fasting, especially James Parnell, who starved to death in Colchester Jail, and John Love, who was probably hanged by the Inquisition at Rome. Parnell's death occurred 10 April 1656, at Colchester. It is probably this to which John Evelyn refers when in his

---

[1] Edward Smith, *The Life of William Dewsbury* (Barclay's Select Series (1836), vol. II, p. 132). Reprinted in *Friends' Library* (Philadelphia (1849), vol. II, pp. 253 f.).

[2] Accordingly Thomas Ellwood frequently omitted them, as he did the miracles; I, 51, James Nayler fasted 14 days; I, 105, Richard Hubberthorne fasted until he was thought to be dead; I, 107, George Fox in a fast about 10 days. These instances were all in 1652 and 1653, as was another fast of Fox of unspecified duration (I, 72). John Toldervy, referring to about the same time, says some Friends 'were limited to fast from food as I remember about twenty or more days together'. 'And afterwards I knew some who fasted 30 or 40 days.' *The Foot out of the Snare* (1656), p. 8. An account in William Caton's letter from Swarthmore Hall 23 Oct. 1659 tells how young and old in that household were fasting, from five to more than twenty days (Swarthmore MSS. IV, 267, quoted in Braithwaite, *Beginnings*, p. 372). But Fox was no indiscriminate admirer of fasting. He says in his *Journal* under date of 1647: 'I heard of a woman in Lancashire that had fasted two and twenty days, and I travelled to see her, but when I came to her I saw that she was under a temptation' (Ellwood, 1694, p. 12; 1891, I, 18).

Diary he describes, under date of 8 July 1656, a visit to Ipswich:

I had the curiosity to visit some Quakers here in prison; a new fanatic sect of dangerous principles who show no respect to any man, magistrate or other, and seem a melancholy proud sort of people and exceedingly ignorant. One of these was said to have fasted twenty days; but another endeavouring to do the like perished on the 10th, when he would have eaten but could not.[1]

From among other references I quote one from a neighbouring Rector, Jeffery Watts, B.D., of Much Leighs, who speaks of 'one James Parnel, a chief and head Quaker in Colchester prison, who as for one while he would drink nothing but water, so another which [*sic*] took upon him to fast 40 days and nights in imitation of Christ. Christ in patience suffered him to go on about ten or eleven days... but after in wrath sent death'.[2]

As an example of such fasts may be cited, instead of any of those mentioned by Fox, the following autobiographical account of Miles Halhead, another of the early Quakers:

Again, the word of the Lord came unto me in the 10th Month, in the Government of Oliver Cromwell, in the year 1652, when I was walking among my sheep, saying, 'Thou shalt not eat nor drink for the space of 14 days anything but water. But fear not for I will feed thee with the dew of heaven, and with the sweet incomes of my love, and my word shall be unto thee sweeter than the honey, or the honey-comb, and I will make thee to know that I am able to keep and preserve thee fresh and strong, and able to do my work without the creatures, as well as with it.' And so in the name of the Lord I set on, and fasted fourteen days without any meat or drink save only water. And indeed the Lord was good unto me, for in all that time I was kept very fresh and able of body, so that no Friend nor other could discern that I wanted either meat or drink.[3]

---

[1] See Braithwaite, *Beginnings*, pp. 191 f., n. In spite of the difference in place (Ipswich), Evelyn's reference to death on the tenth day of fasting corresponds to the verdict procured at the inquest of Parnell of 'wilful rejecting of his natural food for ten days together'.

[2] *A Vindication of the Church and Universities of England* (London, 1657), cited from *The Essex Review* (1909), vol. XVII, p. 186.

[3] *A Book of Some of the Sufferings and Passages of Myles Halhead* (1690), p. 6.

Introduction

Some Friends did not hesitate to challenge their opponents to a fast. In 1655 Richard Farnsworth wrote to Thomas Moor of Boston in Lincolnshire, suggesting that some of the Quakers and some of the chiefest of the people of the Manifestarians in and about Boston and Lynn [Norfolk] should go both of them two weeks without food or drink except a little spring water. As the test was to see which group without artificial food could produce the best preaching, they were also to go without any book all that time.[1]

A similar challenge in 1658 was promulgated by none other than George Fox himself in *An Answer to a Paper which came from the Papists lately out of Holland*. Refuting the idea that Quakers deny the fastings mentioned in the Gospels and the Acts, Fox wrote:

> Many of the Quakers have fasted thirty days, twenty days, fifteen days, ten days, seven days together; I which am a woman (the writer of this) fasted twenty two days, which never none of the Papists fasted forty days, or thirty days, or twenty two days together.[2]

He continues with a challenge:

> I will challenge all the Papists upon the earth, let them come out and go thirty days together without either bread or water, or fourteen days, or twenty days, or let them come out and go thirty days together with nothing but bread and water, and try, and see if his belly be not his God; and the Quakers is known that they never had more strength than when they have fasted two and twenty, and thirty days together.

[1] Watson MSS. 208. Farnsworth's challenge was printed by Moor in *An Antidote against the Spreading Infections of the Spirit of Antichrist* (1655), pp. 8 ff. It and the similar challenges to be mentioned below are most of them cited or quoted extensively by Francis Bugg in *Goliah's Head Cut Off* (1708), 'A Finishing Stroke', pt. IV, § XIX, pp. 298–303. A collection of some of them in a later hand is in the Parrish MSS. at the Historical Society of Pennsylvania.

[2] P. 3. The woman is probably Fox's amanuensis and responsible only for a single clause. It is of course possible that Fox has put his initials to another's work as in other pamphlets.

The challenge is made more prominent and more explicit on the title-page:

And if any Papist in England, or Jesuit, Pope or Cardinal elsewhere, will go forth three or four weeks with a Quaker, with bread and water, and have no more of that then the Quaker hath; for you Papists have said that the Quakers deny fasting; so if you dare try this matter, then some of your side shall watch the Quaker, and some of the Quakers side shall watch you, and so we shall try if your bellies be not your god.

There is no evidence that this challenge was accepted.

A very similar ordeal by fasting was proposed in 1668 by Solomon Eccles in his pamphlet *The Quakers Challeng at Two Several Weapons to the Baptists, Presbiters, Papists and other Professors*. The two weapons were these:

To fast seven days and seven nights and not to eat nor to drink. And the next weapon is: To wake seven days and seven nights and not to sleep till they be faithfully performed before the Lord...and he that the Lord shall carry through this fiery trial shall be counted a worshipper of the true God....But he that tires by the way shall be counted a member of a false church and a heretic.

Mentioning various other sects as well as several individuals by name, Eccles went on to taunt the opponents of Quakerism and to invite them to this duel. He even suggested that after this two times seven was over they should try three times seven more.

There is no evidence that this challenge was accepted at the time or carried out any more than was an earlier duel between Eccles and a certain William Jordan, the Presbyterian from whom he says he had secured a promise of a thirty-nine-day fast. Eccles himself, however, at least gave himself some practice in the two forms of abstinence. During his voyage with Fox and others to America we find the following in John Hull's log book for 23rd of 7 mo. 1671:

This evening Solomon Eccles' seven day fast was out having neither eaten nor drunk all the time, unless sometimes he washed his mouth with vinegar; neither did he go to bed nor hardly slept during the time prefixt, unless now and then he nodded a little at night times as he sat up.[1]

Writing just two years later Solomon Eccles refers to his challenge as still unanswered though he says: 'L. Muggleton and the Baptists have agreed with John Pennyman to get something against S.E. to save their bellies.'[2]

Eccles' printed challenge was finally accepted in print by an equally eccentric man, John Pennyman, himself an ex-Quaker of London. This folio sheet is dated 8 February 1680/1 and is entitled *The Quaker's Challenge* (by Solomon Eccles) *answered, By a Stripling of the Lamb's Army*.[3] Although Eccles is said to have come to London later in 1681 a few weeks before his death, there is no evidence that he either carried out or declined his previous offer.

Fox, perhaps more than his associates, was sensitive to the miraculous aspect of his experience. It took expression in several forms—visions, auditions, insights or foresights, prophecies, escapes from disaster or arrest, recovery from maltreatment of persecutors. The escapes of the Quaker travellers by land in America seemed to Fox miraculous, such as his own survival among the man-eating Indians, or the successful traversing of the wilderness by Josiah Coale. The latter seemed to Fox the exact accomplishment of the very miracle that the New England persecutors challenged the Quakers to show. When they forbade them all access to the colonies by sea, they bade Friends 'to come through the Heathen by land from Virginia to New-England, through the wilderness; for they looked for miracles'.[4] When in 1671 he went to America the ship only barely

---

[1] II, 184.

[2] Paper dated 24 September 1673, printed in William Penn, *Judas and the Jews*, p. 72 (misnumbered for 80).

[3] See Joseph Smith, *A Descriptive Catalogue of Friends' Books* (1867), vol. II, p. 368, item 16. Note also item 17.

[4] Fox, 'Epistle to the Reader' in *The Books and Divers Epistles of Josiah Coale* (1671), p. 21.

escaped capture. In 1677 of the voyage from the Brill to Harwich he writes bluntly in his own hand:

> It was a mirkell [miracle], for we had a great storm and our ship was so leaky that both the pumps could not hardly answer. And the master stopped some leaks in the day time, but in the night the storms was so great and the ship so leaky and the passengers all so sick that the pump went all night. And I had such a travail on my spirit concerning the ship and the people for I saw the people as though they had been all sunk in the sea. And the people was in a pitiful fear, and I desired the Lord God of heaven for his name and truth's sake, who had the winds in his hands and the sea in the hollow of his hands, who could stop the waves [or leaks] and the sea at his pleasure. And the Lord God did answer me, and his power went over all, and his glory did shine over all. And I did hear the pumps suck, and the wind came more fair for us and so we came all safe to Harwich.[1]

An anonymous contemporary agrees very nearly with Fox not only in the spelling of the word 'miracle' but also in the application of it. After telling how in 1661 George Rofe came 'from Maryland in a boat very small, being but fourteen feet by the keel, and landed safe on the south side of Long Island', he adds 'it was a mirkall'.[2]

The form of miracle which is most characteristic of Fox's belief is the cure of disease, both physical and mental. Though it has been noted that Fox mentions none of these things in his earliest writings, and always minimized the evidential importance of visions, foresight and miracles,[3] he came to look back to them as characteristic of the first breaking forth of Truth.

After one of his many accounts of the early cure in 1649 of the distracted woman at Mansfield-Woodhouse, he says:

> Many great and wonderful things were wrought by the heavenly power in those days; for the Lord made bare his omnipotent arm,

---

[1] *Annual Catalogue*, 4, 39 G. This part as well as Penn's milder account of the same storm is printed in Hull, *William Penn and the Dutch Quaker Migration*, pp. 68 f.   [2] *B.F.H.A.* (1946), vol. xxxv, p. 24.

[3] Rachel Hadley King, op. cit. p. 103.

and manifested his power to the astonishment of many, by the healing virtue whereof many have been delivered from great infirmities, and the devils were made subject through his name; of which particular instances might be given, beyond what this unbelieving age is able to receive or hear.[1]

In his testamentary papers written in 1685 he says:

The book in which the Lord's power was manifest at the breaking first of the Truth, where it may be seen some are miracles that his power wrought, you may print if you will.[2]

This writing is not identified, but every later history by him contains miraculous narratives. The *Short Journal* written in Lancaster Jail in 1663–4 apart from his own recovery from bruises and wounds,[3] and his escape from worse disasters[4] mentions at least three early miracles.[5] The *Journal* commonly known as the Spence MSS. or (as published) the Cambridge *Journal,* written in 1674–7 contains many more,[6] while a brief history of Quakerism written just before his death mentions like the *Short Journal* one of his early miracles and adds:

And many miracles the Lord by his power did work which would be tedious to mention all, although we have many upon record.[7]

But beside these incidental references there was once in existence a special collection of such episodes connected with Fox. It was called simply the 'Book of Miracles'. As both references to it in the text of the 1674–7 manuscript *Journal* are insertions,[8] we may conjecture that it was later

[1] *Journal* (1694), p. 28; (1891), i, 45.

[2] ii, 348.

[3] iii, 11, 24, 26, 27.

[4] iii, 47: 'Many miraculous deliverances I had which would make a great volume if they should be declared.'

[5] iii, 2 f., 15, 27; cf. nos. 32 *b*, 31 *b*, 60 *b*.

[6] See ii, 511, 'Remarkable Cures'; 519, 'Miracles'; adding references to ii, 153, 313 and 342.

[7] MS. entitled 'How the Lord by his Power and Spirit did Raise up Friends'.

[8] ii, 106, 313. The insertions are in the same hand as the original MS. The second implies it was among the books written or collected at Swarthmore Hall about 1675.

III. Instructions in Hand of George Fox for Printing his Miracles and other Works

(*See* page 39)

than that date. On the other hand, apparently the History just quoted, which was written in 1689, refers to it as then extant. As we shall see, it included events as late as 1685, and may well have been compiled after that date. If the phrase in the testamentary papers of 1685 quoted above refers to the 'Book of Miracles' it would give us a *terminus ante quem* for dating it, but the identification is doubtful.[1] At any rate in 1694 or thereabouts when the materials for the *Annual Catalogue* were being collected there was at London a book so entitled. It was in manuscript in folio size, and it was bound. Though it is not catalogued itself as a whole it was entered extensively in the index.

In his testamentary papers of 1685 Fox made provision for the printing of his works. He names thirteen Friends to have charge of the task, he mentions the sources of money which are to pay not only for the printing but for some free distribution, and he indicates the location and character of the material available both printed and in manuscript. Except for the item already quoted, these papers mention neither miracles nor a book of miracles. There is, however, a briefer and probably earlier instruction by Fox on publication, in which he outlines a three-fold collection of his works and specifically mentions miracles in the first division. In a large folio volume into which various of his papers had been copied about 1681, and in which after his death the elaborate *Annual Catalogue* and index were compiled,[2] Fox wrote in his own hand:

This book is to be printed with the rest of g ff in 3 voulames: 1: his epeseles & merrekeles & leters & travels & books without contreverce that are ansers 2 & all the ansers & contreverces by them seveles 3 all the bookes of noates & as this booke is & the generall papers to the men & wimens meetings by them seveles.

Fox left to his executors all decision on publication, and they took considerable liberty to omit or to edit. They took their task seriously as we know, not merely by the

---

[1] The identification is assumed by Brayshaw, op. cit. p. 171.
[2] See my edition of the *Annual Catalogue*, p. 5, item indicated as Aa.

three large volumes that they published in 1694, 1698 and
1706, but by minutes and memoranda recording their
discussions and intentions. The 'Book of Miracles' must
have been known to them. Apparently they once made
a minute about it, now lost.[1] Since they never concluded the original plan for a complete edition of Fox's
works, it is possible that the publication of the 'Book of
Miracles' was not vetoed but merely postponed. There
were, however, good reasons for a cautious attitude to
the subject. Like Fox himself, his friends knew that
such claims could be abused, and were subject to
ridicule. And they would not seem to rest their case on
such credentials. They probably did not want Fox's
friends to imitate or his enemies to criticize such achieve-
ments.

This attitude of caution can be shown from their treatment of his *Journal*. Both references to the 'Book of
Miracles' in the manuscript were omitted by Ellwood who
edited it under the direction of the Morning Meeting and
several of the narrative miracles which were in the MS.
were entirely omitted. For example under date of 1653,
following his release from Carlisle prison, Fox related four
cures which belonged to that neighbourhood and perhaps
to that time. They are all omitted by Ellwood. For the
omission of the first two, another editorial aversion well
attested elsewhere—against excessive adoration of Fox—
could have been responsible as will be seen from the
text:

And after I came out of Carlisle prison aforesaid I went into the
Abbey chamber. And there came in a mad woman that sometimes
was very desperate, and she fell down of her knees, and cried, 'Put
off your hats! for grace hangs about thy neck.' And so the Lord's
power run through her that she was sensible of her condition, and
after came and confessed it to Friends.

And I came to another place in Cumberland where a man's wife
was distracted and very desperate, attempting at times to kill her
children and her husband, but I was moved of the Lord God to

[1] See below, p. 64 n. 1.

40

speak to her, and she kneeled down of her bare knees and cried and said she would work of her bare knees if she might go with me. And the Lord's power wrought through her and she went home well.[1]

But the other two miracles related here, and others omitted by Ellwood, were objected to on other grounds.

Other evidence of editorial reserve may be found in some of the minor changes of wording. The parallels, printed below with differences italicized, indicate apparently a tendency to reduce the publicity, the immediacy, and the semi-magical nature of the cures and to emphasize faith, prayer, and the power of God, rather than giving credit to men.

Cambridge *Journal*	Ellwood, 1694
I, 108: And he stood up and stretcht out his arm which had been lame a long time and said, be it known unto you all people *and to all nations*, that this day I am healed.	103: And he stood up and stretched out his arm that had been lame a long time and said, Be it known unto you, all people, that this day I am healed.
I, 201: And I was sent for to her, and the Lord raised her up again and settled her mind by his power.	171: Then was I sent for to her and the Lord *was entreated and* raised her up again and settled her mind by his power.
II, 229: He was finely raised up & after came to our meetings . . . the man being much refreshed when I left him.	373: [I] spake what the Lord gave me to him; and the man was much refreshed and finely raised up *by the power of the Lord*; and he afterwards came to our meetings.

---

[1] I, 140. For Ellwood's omissions of features in the Spence MSS. see I, pp. xv–xxviii, and T. Edmund Harvey, *The Journals of George Fox* (a paper read before the London Society for the Study of Religion 5 Dec. 1911, and privately printed). The text of other miracles omitted by Ellwood will be found repeated here and there throughout this study.

Cambridge *Journal*	Ellwood, 1694
II, 234: Thus Captain Batts told me *and had spread it up and down in the country among the people*. And he asked me of it and I said many things had been done by the power of Christ.	376: And he desired to know the certainty of it. I told him *we did not glory in such things*; but many such things had been done by the power of Christ.
II, 243: So I was moved to go to her and tell her that salvation was come to her house and did speak other words to her and for her and *that hour* she mended . . . and is well; blessed be the Lord!	381: When I heard of her I was moved *of the Lord* to go to her and tell her, that salvation was come to her house. And after I had spoken the word *of life* to her and *intreated the Lord* for her she mended . . . and is *since* well: blessed be the Lord!
II, 310: When I was there before she desired me to *lay my hands on her and* pray for her, which I did and it was *immediately* made well.	407: When I was there before she had brought her to me . . . and had then desired me to pray for her; which I did, and she grew well upon it, *praised be the Lord*.
III, 78: And as I laid my hand upon him the Lord's power went through him, *and his wife was sensible of the thing,* and he presently fell off asleep . . . but the Lord's power in his time soon gave him ease.	504: And as I laid my hand on him the Lord's power went through him and *through faith in that power* he had speedy ease so that he quickly fell into a sleep. . . . But the Lord *was intreated for him* and by his power soon gave him ease at this time.

One miracle story appeared in the second folio volume of his works, *The Epistles*, published in 1698. A somewhat long historic account, occurring in the Spence MSS. but omitted in the *Journal*, was used as prefatory matter.[1] And it contains the following:

[1] Pp. 2–7. It was included in some later editions of Fox's *Journal* in a briefer form, e.g. 1891, II, 251–4. From the Spence MSS. it is transcribed in II, 338–44.

Introduction

And at one time I was sent for to White Chapel; about the third hour in the morning to a woman that was dying and her child, and the people was weeping about her. And after a while I was moved (in the name and power of Christ Jesus) to speak to the woman. And she and her child was raised up. And she got up to the astonishment of the people when they came in, in the morning, and her child was also healed.[1]

But it was in the *Journal*, published in 1694, that in spite of the editor's restraint, Fox disclosed his belief in his miraculous power. No less than twelve episodes of the sort were allowed to remain in the text, and were boldly listed in the index as 'Miracles'. Even here the editor has shown certain care to attribute the power to the Creator rather than to the creature. I transcribe the whole entry:

Miracles wrought by the Power of God, 167. She that was ready to die, raised up again, 170, 171. The Lame made whole, 103. The Diseased restored, 407. A distracted Woman healed, 27, 28 (see *Trouble* of *Mind*). A great Man given over by Physicians, restored, 30, 258. *G.F.* prays for a Woman ready to die, 70, and for a distracted Woman at *Chichester*, 171. Restores John Jay's Neck broke (as the People said) by a fall from an Horse in *East-Jersey*, 370, 371. Speaks to a Sick-man in *Mary-land*, who was raised up by the Power of the Lord, 373. and prays the Lord to rebuke *J.C.*'s Infirmity, and the Lord by his Power soon gave him Ease, &c., 503, 504.

The cross-reference is

Troubles of Mind spoken to, 189. Of a woman in *Maryland*, for whom *G.F.* intreated the Lord, 381.

Readers of the *Journal* ever since its publication have noted these passages. They were objected to by the critics

---

[1] *Epistles* (1698), p. 6 (*Works* (1831), vol. VII, p. 14). The MS. does not have the words 'in the name and power of Christ Jesus', nor 'when they came in, in the morning'.

The date of the episode is not given, but it was followed next day by the establishment in London of a weekly meeting of sixty women who were to visit the sick. That was apparently in one of the last years of the Protectorate. See below, pp. 46–7.

of Fox or of Quakerism, like Charles Leslie[1] and Samuel Newton[2] and by various ex-Quakers like Francis Bugg.[3] They have been defended, admired or discussed by Fox's friends, admirers or biographers.[4]

Thomas Ellwood who edited the *Journal* makes no reference to miraculous powers in his brief eulogy of the author.[5] Nor does William Penn in his much longer and more famous preface refer to the miracles, though he must have known those contained in the *Journal* and probably those omitted from the original manuscript as well. Neither Ellwood nor Penn mentions the 'Book of Miracles' or suggests its publication, but Penn does mention a similar collection, the Quaker prophecies of the future which came to be fulfilled adding that 'in time they be made publick for the Glory of God'. It is just possible that in the phrase he uses of Fox 'a Divine and a Naturalist, and all of God Almighty's making', naturalist includes the medical element in natural philosophy, just as Manasseh

---

[1] *The Snake in the Grass* (1696), pp. lxiv f. *A Parallel between the Faith and Doctrine of the Present Quakers and that of the Chief Heretics* (1707), p. 48 (an item not in his collected works nor listed in Jos. Smith's *Bibliotheca Anti-quakeriana*), where Fox's miracles are compared with those claimed by the Papists.

[2] *The Leading Sentiments of the People Called Quakers Examined* (1771), pp. 27–32; cf. p. 101. This was answered by Joseph Phipps, *The Original and Present State of Man, Briefly Considered* (1773, and many later editions), ch. XIII, § 5.

[3] See below, pp. 85–91. Cf. E[dward] A[sh], *George Fox, his Character, Doctrine and Work* (1873), pp. 17 f.

[4] Samuel M. Janney, *The Life of George Fox* (1853), pp. 115–18; *History of the Religious Society of Friends* (1861), vol. II, pp. 286–9. A. C. Bickley, *George Fox and the Early Quakers* (1884), pp. 103 ff. Frederick Storrs Turner, *The Quakers: a Study Historical and Critical* (1889), ch. VIII. A. Neave Brayshaw, *The Personality of George Fox* (1919), pp. 45 f., 83–6, and much more fully in an enlarged edition (1933), pp. 90–2, 167–78. Edward Grubb, 'Spiritual Healing Among the Early Friends', *The Venturer* (1916), vol. I, pp. 212–15, 236–9, reprinted in his *Quaker Thought and History* (1925), pp. 149–67. 'George Fox and Spiritual Healing', *The Friend* (London, 1924), vol. LXIV, pp. 600–1. John William Graham, *The Divinity in Man* (1927), pp. 240–4. Howard E. Collier, M.D., 'Miracles and Healings during the First Period of Quakerism', *Friends Quarterly Examiner* (1944), vol. LXXVIII, pp. 280–8 and 'George Fox's Practice', ibid. (1945), vol. LXXIX, pp. 28–35.

[5] Pp. xvi f.

ben Israel on the title-page of his address *To His Highness the Lord Protector* (1655), designates himself 'a Divine and Doctor of Physick'. There are, however, other meanings for naturalist. One misunderstanding akin to the miraculous claim of cures Penn does recognize and refute. While the Quakers held and taught perfection and freedom from sin, Penn explains that 'they never held a perfection in wisdom and glory in this life, or from natural infirmities or death, as some have with a weak or ill mind imagined or insinuated against them'. Though Sewel in his *History* used extensively Fox's printed *Journal*, it has been noted that Sewel relates but very few miracles.

GEORGE FOX, MIRACLE AND MEDICINE

There are several aspects of Fox's attitude which prevent his belief in miracles from becoming extreme miracle-mongering or even gross egotism. The incidents verge on the one hand upon naturalistic medical cures, on the other upon purely spiritual services of sympathy and encouragement.

It was natural that his friends and admirers should long for his presence and should anticipate comfort and strength from his visit. An early letter from his lifelong friend Robert Widders to Margaret Fell is typical. It runs in part:

Upon the last third day at night I was terribly shaken in my body and a little after I was taken with a stitch in my right side which was exceeding much pain to the outward man...now I am even burnt up like a parched wilderness...I never had such a trial as this before, and let thy prayers be to the living God for me that whether it be life or death the Lord may be honoured by me. Oh that I might see thy face this day, I believe I should be refreshed. Or oh that G.F. were free to come over this night, I have some hope to be restored to my former joy again....[1]

---

[1] Swarthmore MSS. I, 43 (spelling modernized). George Fox has dated this as 1652. Robert and Jane Widders lived at Over Kellet, across the sands from Swarthmore. Fox's letter of sympathy to them on the death of their son Robert in 1676 unfortunately is not preserved as a whole. See *Annual Catalogue*, 82 F.

Introduction

It is obvious, especially from the *Itinerary Journals*,[1] how usual it was for Fox to visit the sick. For him this was a part of his pastoral service. In fact there was so much of it to be done that he organized in London a group of sixty women to meet once a week

that they might see and inquire into the necessity of all poor Friends, who were sick and weak and were in wants, or widows and fatherless in the city and suburbs...and that they in visiting the sick in the Lord's power and word, through which they would have the wisdom of the Lord, and of his creation and how to administer his creatures and by the same power to heal and strengthen with the outward things and without them; which they have felt prosperous to this day. And great things have been done in their meetings by the Lord's power.[2]

In Fox's vocabulary creation, creatures and outward things refer to *materia medica*. The meeting was to provide a large-scale 'ministry of healing'.

The same connection between miracles and women's meetings for the care of the poor seems to be in Fox's mind when in speaking to the women Friends at Barbados he said: 'So Friends will come to the understanding in the Creation. I believe there is a thousand women [Friends] that are beyond the wisdom of the world all: yea, and the power of God hath wrought miracles among them who keep their minds and hearts pure and holy to

[1] See III, 75 (a man and a woman Friend that was ill), 82 (Mary Woolley), 89 (Margaret Rous), 90 (a woman at Ellington not well in her mind), 100 (Giles Fettiplace), 104 (a Friend that lay sick in Houndsditch, a prisoner of Newgate), 117 (George Whitehead's wife's sister), etc. Ellwood (1694), p. 513; (1891), II, 389, condenses one such period by having Fox say: 'sometimes also visiting those that were sick and weak in body, or troubled in mind, helping to bear their spirits up from sinking under their infirmities'. Cf. ibid. (1694), pp. 519, 550, 563, 576; (1891), II, pp. 396, 434, 449, 463.

[2] II, 342 f. (=*Epistles*, p. 6). Fox speaks of this plan as having been opened to him in connection with his cure of the woman and her daughter in White Chapel (see above, p. 43), 'when I was sent for to many sick people'. No full minutes of this women's meeting are extant to show whether the women claimed to work miracles. Some of them are mentioned elsewhere as being cured, e.g. Mariabella Farmborough (p. 16) and Mary Elson (no. 64 a).

46

God.'[1] Referring probably to still earlier times Fox mentions many meetings and many miracles at the house of Elizabeth Hooton at Skegby, Notts.[2]

Of the establishment of the London meeting of women Friends, other accounts are given later by Gilbert Latey and by Mary Elson. The latter, who had long been a member, writes:

> And our dear Friend George Fox... was many times sent for to many that were weak and sick in this city... and he was moved of the Lord to advise a women's meeting, and in order thereto he sent for such women as he knew in this City.... Dear G. Fox declared unto us what the Lord had made known unto him by his power that there should be a women's meeting, that so all the sick, the weak, the widdows and the fatherless should be minded and looked after.[3]

Only in the most remote sense can such activities be associated with modern planning for public health. As Auguste Jorns has written:

> Even the first Quakers did no more, so far as can be definitely ascertained, than meet the exigencies of physical need and offer

---

[1] 28 October 1671 at the house of Thomas Rous. See *Annual Catalogue*, 8, 23 F.

[2] See below, p. 60.

[3] *A True Information of our Blessed Women's Meeting*, p. 11. The same essay refers to this meeting as being gathered betwixt twenty three and twenty four years ago'. But the essay itself is not dated and Ann Whitehead's *Epistle of True Love and Unity* with which it is printed was published by Andrew Sowle without date. That is usually assigned to 1680 but the two pages of advertisement at the end of 'books printed and sold by Andrew Sowle' include dated imprints of 1681, 1682 and 1683, and this piece probably belongs to the last of these years. This would fix the date of the meeting's origin about 1658 or 1659.

M. G. Swift in *Bulletin of Friends' Historical Society* (1910), vol. III, p. 151, arrives at the same date on the basis of some details in an account of the meeting's origin written by Gilbert Latey in 1705. The date is discussed by Beck and Ball, *London Friends' Meetings*, p. 347, and Braithwaite, *Beginnings of Quakerism*, pp. 341 f. The matter is perhaps confused by the existence shortly afterwards of another women's meeting in London, which is also mentioned by Mary Elson and discussed in the books just cited. I am not sure that Fox and Latey (*Brief Narrative of the Life and Death of... Gilbert Latey* (1707), pp. 145–7) are talking of the same meeting.

religious consolation. The miraculous cures that Fox tells about—they agree very closely with those recorded in the Bible—cannot be clearly judged; they have nothing in common with the systematic care of the sick. There is even a certain amount of contempt of medical skill to be felt—prayer and laying on of hands prove effective, where the doctors fail. But this too is not surprising. Of what significance was the science of the world in comparison with the power of faith![1]

That Fox did not ignore the use of natural remedies is indicated by his reference to the 'creation', 'creatures', and 'outward things' in the passage already quoted and by plentiful evidence elsewhere. A knowledge of the virtue (i.e. curative properties) of herbs was opened to him at the time of his conversion so that he says: 'I was at a stand in my mind whether I should practice physic for the good of mankind, seeing the nature and virtues of the creatures were so opened to me by the Lord.'[2]

In middle life Fox included a knowledge of herbs in his plans for education. He wrote to William Penn in 1674 proposing a school in the country near London, where the instruction in classics by Richard Richardson, 'who is a man rather to fit scholars rather than pupil them', would be supplemented by the practical advice of Thomas Lawson. The latter refers years later to this plan for a garden schoolhouse, and his intention in this connection to compile a book on plants. He actually established a school at Great Strickland in Westmorland. In 1675 a minute of the Six Weeks Meeting in London refers to 'the proposition made by G. F. touching Wm. Thomlinson's setting up a school to teach the languages, etc. together with the nature of flowers, roots, plants and trees'. While we have no evidence that the projects near London came into being in Fox's time, the ideal remained among Friends. John Bellers in 1695 in his famous *Proposals for Raising a*

---

[1] *The Quakers as Pioneers in Social Work* (Engl. tr. 1931), pp. 144 f. She continues by contrasting John Bellers' later *Essay towards the Improvement of Physick* (1714).

[2] *Journal* (1694), p. 18; (1891), I, 28.

Colledge of Industry included 'a library of books, a physic-garden for understanding of herbs, and a laboratory for preparing of medicines'.[1] And late in life Fox in bequeathing to Friends in Philadelphia a piece of land, intended part of it 'for a garden, and to be planted with all sorts of physical plants, for lads and lasses to learn simples there, and the uses to convert them to—distilled waters, oils, ointments, etc.'[2]

On one occasion at least a cure attributed to Fox was due to medicine—if that is what 'things' means in the following reference to an illness of Edward Pyott near Bristol.

> Edward was a dying man to all appearance when we came first to his house and George ordered him to take things; and he was subject to him and now he is fine and well. His ague hath left him. The thing is much noised amongst Friends, he being before so weak and no likelihood of his life.[3]

[1] P. 20. For earlier items in this paragraph, see *J.F.H.S.* (1910), vol. VII, p. 74; S. F. Locker Lampson, *The Quaker Post-Bag*, pp. 20–3; A. N. Brayshaw, *The Personality of George Fox* (1933), p. 114.

[2] Webb, *Fells* (1896), p. 393. Cf. *B.F.H.S.* (1909), vol. III, pp. 100 f. The ideals of Fox were perhaps never better fulfilled among his followers than by Josiah White (1705–80) of Mt Holly, New Jersey. Without scientific training in botany he acquired an extraordinary reputation as having insight into the use of indigenous roots and herbs. In fact the insight extended to an ability to know where sick persons were to be found who needed his assistance. 'His applications were simple but almost miraculously certain in their effect in overcoming the disease, and often where the patient had been thought incurable. He has been known frequently to call at houses both in Philadelphia and in the country as he passed along, where he was a total stranger, and inquire if some one was not sick. Nor was the impulse of his mind thus directed ever known to mislead him.' See his Memoirs in *Friends' Weekly Intelligencer* (1846), vol. III, pp. 265 f. Cf. *The Friend* (Philadelphia, 1886–7), vol. LX, pp. 162 f.

[3] John Stubbs to Margaret Fell, Bristol, 28th of 5 mo. 1662 in II, 22; quoted also in 1838 in Elisha Bates, *Appeal to the Society of Friends*, p. 23. In Ellwood's *Journal* (1694), p. 254; (1891), I, 528, the passage is abbreviated and put into Fox's mouth as follows: 'Edward was brought so low and weak with an ague, that when I came first thither he was looked upon as a dying man: but it pleased the Lord to raise him up again so that before I went away, his ague left him and he was finely well.' Ellwood does not indicate, as Stubbs' letter does, that Dr Bourne was with Bristol Friends on this occasion. Had he prescribed the 'things'?

During his residence at Swarthmore Hall medicines were bought frequently for both man and beast.[1] An itemized bill, paid 5 August 1676, includes among different quantities either, of brandy or of stomach waters for several members of the family, '4 quarts of brandy for father...4s.'[2] Another bill paid two years earlier was to Thomas Lawson, the famous herbalist, himself a Friend, for instruction given to Thomas Lower and the women of the Swarthmore household in the medicinal use of herbs.[3]

A decade later in listing property to be distributed to his heirs Fox names several items that are probably medical:

> my sea case with the glass bottles in it,...will hold some liquor or drink if any should be faint.
> my little case with the bottles in it, that is covered with straw all my physical things that came from beyond the sea
> my other little trunk that standeth in Benjamin Antrobus' closet with the outlandish things in it (my little trunk at BA and all my phisical things in it or elsewhere)
> the outlandish cup
> that thing that people do give glisters with (a glister pipe)[4].

The first item was to be a kind of 'first aid' store at Swarthmore Meeting House, but most of these objects

---

[1] See *Household Account Book of Sarah Fell* (edited by Norman Penney, 1920), index, s.v. 'Medicine'. Many other references to medicine occur, but are not indexed.

[2] Ibid. p. 299.

[3] Ibid. p. 95, last entry, but n. 3 is lacking.

In his unpublished account of Friends Fox speaks of 'Thomas Lawson who was a priest and scholar and is one of the greatest simplers in England'. A good many years later John Rodes, a young Quaker of social position received a letter in which he is told that Thomas Lawson offered to teach him among other subjects 'Latine and Greek and instruct him in the product of plants'. Lawson's own letter which is preserved explains his previous study of botany and his idea of an herbarium. S. F. Locker Lampson, *A Quaker Post-Bag* (1910), pp. 19 ff. On Lawson, see *D.N.B.*

[4] II, 351–60. A 'clyster pipe' or syringe. See illustration opposite.

The 'physical' things may of course be related not to physic (medicine) but to physics in the modern sense, i.e. curiosities like the magnifying glass mentioned in these bequests and still extant at the Historical Society of Pennsylvania; but in contemporary English I think the medical meaning is more probable.

This High-German Doctor, Cured the Emperor of *Turk*'s Brother, who was Blind 13 Years.

IV. The High-German Doctor Operating for Blindness

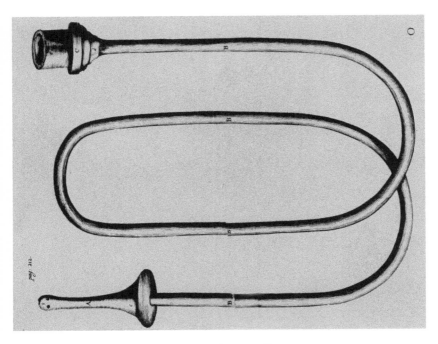

V. A Clyster Pipe

were appropriately left to the one of his heirs who was a doctor, Thomas Lower.[1]

Ten years later a list was made of more than 100 books formerly owned by Fox but then at the home of another son-in-law, William Meade, in London. One of them was the widely circulated handbook of home medicine, Nicholas Culpeper's *The English Physitian Enlarged*.[2]

Fox's confidence in doctors and medicines is further attested by another member of the Swarthmore household many years earlier. Margaret Fell the younger, writing from London to her mother 13 March 1660, refers to a course of baths for her knee made with herbs and of her intention of consulting a Dutchman about it as advised by George Fox.[3]

Fox felt some doubt whether the professional doctors really understood the secrets of their profession. In his early experiences it was opened to him 'that the physicians were out of the wisdom of God by which the creatures were made and so knew not their virtues'.[4] More than once he propounded queries on this subject. In 1657 questions drawn up at Lyme Regis at night and left behind to be stuck upon the Market Cross are described as dealing with 'the ground of all diseases, and whether Adam or Eve had any before they fell, and whether there was any in the restoration by Christ Jesus again, and whether any knew the virtue of all the creatures in the creation whose virtue and nature was according to its first name, except they was in the wisdom of God by which they was made and

[1] On the extent of Lower's training and practice as a doctor see the note on 'Thomas Lower's Medical Degree' in L. V. Hodgkin, *A Quaker Saint of Cornwall* (1927), pp. 225 f.

[2] *J.F.H.S.* (1931), vol. xxviii, pp. 2, 7, 15. To judge from some twenty-four of these books which are actually extant, Fox's copy had his initials upon it, and would show written in ink on the fore leaves its number in this list, viz. 75.

[3] Leek MSS. It would be interesting to know who was the Dutchman, perhaps one of the German doctors mentioned elsewhere, though I think some Netherlander is more likely.

[4] Ellwood (1694), p. 18; (1891), i, 29. Cf. 'Book of Miracles', no. 32 *a*.

created'.[1] In the same year he addressed to some scholars, including six doctors of physic, a series of questions, of which two are of the same tendency, viz.:

22. All you that be physicians and doctors, have you the wisdom by which all things was made? Have you the knowledge of the virtue of all the creatures in the creation? Minister you physick by the course and order of the stars and planets? Must the ground of the planet in the man be removed before the ground of the disease be removed, or before he come to the glory of the first body?

24. And what is the ground of mother, stone and colic? and what is the cause of them? and whether or no they do proceed from one root? and how they do differ in their operation and working? and what is the door that lets them in, that they come to be bred?[2]

Written queries as a form of controversy or of self-discipline were characteristic of the period. It is perhaps only a coincidence that we have also from Lyme Regis in 1657 in the Church Book of the Baptists there, or as they are styled, 'the assembly of Protestant dissenters who scrupled the baptizing of infants', the similar question: 'Whether astrology in physicke be lawful.' The written answer of the ministers urges waiting for light on the matter but gives a threefold warning against the evil implicit in the practice.[3]

It would not have been surprising if Fox had rebelled against doctors and the use of physic altogether, and probably some other Friends did so. Of William Coats-

---

[1] I, 269. Ellwood adds, 'and the nature and virtues of medicinable creatures'—a correct interpretation. For the 'first name', cf. *Journal* (Ellwood, 1694), p. 18: 'The creation was opened to me, and it was showed me how all things had their names given them according to their nature and virtue.'

[2] *Here are Several Queries put forth in Print* (1657), p. 6. 'Mother' in this context means fits of hysteria. It was accompanied often by feelings of suffocation and was possibly epilepsy. See W. A. Brend, *Transactions of the Medico-Legal Society* (1907–8), vol. v, pp. 152 f. 'Planet' is also the name of a disease, probably paralysis.

[3] See T. W. Marsh, *Some Records of the Early Friends in Surrey and Sussex* (1886), p. 121. On the Church Book of Lyme Regis, see George Roberts, *The History and Antiquities of Lyme Regis* (1834), pp. 218 f. and *The Baptist Quarterly* (1936), vol. VIII, pp. 44–8.

worth, a Friend of South Shields, who died untimely in 1657, George Whitehead tells us that the doctors 'gave him physick several times until he was near his end; some reported he had physick given him within an hour before he died, though he had before denied the use of such *Carnal Means* (as he termed them) '.[1] So Andrew Brothers of Dorney, Bucks, whose difficulties moral, medical and mental, apparently merged into each other and claimed the patient attention of his Monthly Meeting nearly every month for four years (1686–90), was offered assistance 'if he would put himself into the hands of some skilful physician for the recovery of his health: yet utterly refused to admit of any physical administration, saying unless he were bound in his bed and forced, he should not take anything'.[2]

During an illness in 1670–1, Fox says: 'Several Friends that were doctors came and they would have given me physic, but I was not to meddle with their things.'[3]

But Fox and the early Quakers were not opposed to the medical profession as some faith-healing sects have been. Evidently Fox felt respect for doctors who were not Friends and they in turn were attracted to him. There are several references in his later journals to his meeting 'the King's Chirurgeon' or other doctors. For example, for 26 September 1686 we have this entry: 'He stayed that night [at Thomas Cox's in London] and had discourse with

---

[1] *The Christian Progress of...George Whitehead* (1725), p. 129. The name is spelled also Cotsworth.

[2] Beatrice S. Snell, *The Minute Book of the Monthly Meeting...for the Upperside of Buckinghamshire* (1937), p. 201, and index, s.v. 'Melancholia'.

[3] II, 165 f. Ellwood (1694, p. 342; 1891, II, 131) for 'things' says 'any of their medicines'. With the language compare William Bayly, *The Lamb's Government* (1663), p. 19 (*Works*, p. 345): 'Israel is commanded not to meddle with physick, or physitians.' But neither the Old Testament nor Apocrypha contains such a command. Contrast Ecclus. xxxviii. 4.

The situation is a little different when Katharine Evans 'had not freedom to receive anything' from the physician that was brought to her by the Inquisition authorities that imprisoned her. (*This is a Short Relation* (1662), pp. 10 f.; *A Brief History* (1715), p. 21.)

a great doctor of physic that night and the next morning
who was very friendly and glad of the opportunity with
him.'[1]

Especially interesting are the continental doctors whom
he met. Mention is made elsewhere of two of these who
came to England and became Friends, Albertus Otto Faber
and Francis Mercurius van Helmont. The latter was at
least once in the company of George Fox, at Ragley in
1678 at the house of Lady Conway, and apparently to
mutual satisfaction.[2] In 1660 a German doctor in London,
who had met Fox, wrote to him a letter still preserved
expressing his desire to have his wife meet Fox or hear him
speak.[3] In 1677 one of Fox's hearers when he and William
Penn were at Harlingen in Holland was a doctor of physic,
who later came back to talk to Penn.[4] In January 1686 in
London Fox 'sent for a great doctor that came from
Poland'. None of these men are named. The last of them,
who according to Norman Penney 'has not appeared in any
place in which we have searched for him', is perhaps 'the
eminent doctor of physick newly come out of Poland'
whose portrait and professional claims are known to us
from his own bill of advertisement.[5]

Instead of giving up the medical profession, Quakers

---

[1] III, 154. See also III, 300, for a list of such references.

[2] III, 267. Later Fox criticized some of van Helmont's writings, but they
had to do with occult rather than with medical matters. See *Annual Catalogue*,
19, 93 G and Ji on p. 6. We have evidence that Fox and van Helmont were
guests together in March 1683 at the house of James Claypoole, in a letter
from the last-named to Benjamin Furly. See *Pennsylvania Magazine of
History* (1886), vol. x, p. 269.

[3] Swarthmore MSS. III, 125. This is probably Albertus Otto Faber. See
below, p. 73. He is called a German doctor by others and even in his own
advertisements. Henry Lampe, M.D. (1660–1711) of Königsberg, was
another German doctor who joined Friends in England somewhat later.
His autobiography edited by Joseph J. Green and published in 1895 gives
a vivid picture of the adventures of a doctor and apothecary in Holland,
France, Ireland and England.

[4] III, 248 f.

[5] III, 129, 332. C. J. S. Thompson, *The Quacks of Old London* (1928),
pp. 163 f. In September 1689 'The King's Chirurgeon' came to Fox at
Hampton Wick, possibly, as Penney suggests, 'one who came over with
William III from Holland. Dutch doctors were famous at this Epoch'—III,

who were doctors apparently attempted to discover the special bearing of their faith upon their occupation. Such trade meetings were held by tailors who were Quakers, by shoemakers, by carpenters, by vintners and by school-masters. Each of these occupations made special demands upon a consistent Friend and Fox had a hand in encouraging such meetings.[1] And it would not be surprising if the many Friends who were doctors were occasionally in conference in the same way. So at least I understand the reference in Fox's *Journal* to his 'meeting with the physicians at James Wasse's' in London on 1 June 1683.[2] Only one other reference to such trade meetings is known to me. That is at Barbados where throughout its history on the island Quakerism supplied an unusual number of doctors and where in 1679 a bequest was made by a Friend of a small sum of money to 'the Chirurgeons' Meeting'.[3]

348. The same may be said of Germans. 'London was overrun with German quacks at that time' (G. de Francesco, *The Power of the Charlatan* (1939), p. 109). It is needless to add that royal patronage, real or fictitious, was regarded as an advertising asset.

[1] The evidence for these trade meetings is most abundant in Ireland. See Isabel Grubb, *Friends and Industry*. For the meetings of vintners and publicans, see A. N. Brayshaw, *The Personality of George Fox* (1933), pp. 98 f. (London); for one of schoolmasters, see *Bulletin of Friends' Historical Association* (1940), vol. XXIX, p. 100 (Barbados).

[2] III, 80. On James Wasse (1638–1712) the Quaker and chirurgeon, see III, 300. According to his own advertisement in which he says he 'resolved to publish the Virtues, use and dose of his famous Elixir', he retired to the country after forty years of experience. See Thompson, op. cit. p. 97.

'James Wasse of London, citizen and barber chirurgeon', appears also among property owners in West Jersey having received a patent from John Fenwick 12 July 1675 for 5000 acres confirmed by a deed in 1681 from the successors to Fenwick's title (*New Jersey Archives* (1st ser.), vol. XXI, pp. 397, 564). Later he is spoken of as owning half of one share of the colony (ibid. p. 513). He was one of those entrusted in 1676 by Wm. Penn and the other Friends who had secured an interest in the colony with buying the land from the Indians and otherwise organizing the colony, having gone to Maryland in Samuel Groome's ship, in which also he expected to return (Samuel Smith, *The History of the Colony of Nova-Caesaria, or New Jersey* (1765), pp. 80 f.).

[3] Will of Robert Taylor, Copies of Wills, vol. XIV, p. 101, at the Registry, Bridgetown. From the same time and place comes not merely mention of a meeting of Quaker midwives, but the minutes of several sessions (*J.F.H.S.* (1940), vol. XXXVII, pp. 22–4).

Introduction

While the first generations of Friends may have included several University-trained doctors, the long-continued exclusion of Nonconformists from the Universities automatically curtailed thereafter their later participation in this profession in England, as it would have excluded them from law and divinity had they had no scruples against those professions. They could study medicine in the continental and later in the Scottish Universities; and in the American colonies such stringent regulations for license were not in effect. My impression is that in some of these colonies, notably Barbados, Friends supplied more than their proportion of the medical men. And even in Great Britain several Friends, too numerous to mention here, have achieved distinction in this field in successive generations.[1]

It may be worthwhile to remind the modern reader that in seventeenth-century England unprofessional medical attention was more widely distributed than to-day. Household remedies and recipes were part of the domestic economy, as much as food. Some women excelled in their knowledge and use of herbs or simples. We may mention out of the circle preceding Friends, the mother of William Penn and the grandmother of his wife. Lady Penn left behind her an extensive collection of recipes part medical, part culinary, copies of which prepared apparently for her son are extant in manuscript.[2] Of Lady Springett, Mary Penington, her daughter-in-law, gives in her reminiscences a very attractive picture.[3] They were followed in this capacity by Gulielma Maria Springett of whom a contemporary mentions 'the great cures she does, having great

---

[1] See the articles by David J. Davis, *Bull. Soc. Med. Hist. Chicago* (1928), vol. IV, pp. 77–93; Sir George Newman, *Friends' Quarterly Examiner* (1930), vol. LXIV, pp. 57–70; Cyril C. Barnard, ibid. (1937), vol. LXXI, pp. 307–26 and (1938), vol. LXXII, pp. 68–86.

[2] Penn Manuscripts in Historical Society of Pennsylvania. A few extracts are printed in *Pennsylvania Magazine of History and Biography* (1916), vol. XL, pp. 472–9.

[3] Op. cit. pp. 73–7. Cf. Maria Webb, *Penns and Peningtons* (1877), pp. 61–3.

skill in physic and surgery, which she freely bestows'.[1]
Still preserved in the family is the manuscript book of
household recipes compiled by Christian Barclay (1647–
1722), wife of Robert Barclay, the apologist: 'A Receipt
Book, or the fruits of a young Woman's Spare Hours. Into
three parts, the first containing several receipts of
Physicke, the second concerning Cookerie, and the Third
of dying [i.e., dyeing] very necessary and profitable.'[2]
Mary Mollineux (1651–1695) 'had a good understanding in
physic and surgery...giving both advice and medicines
to them that stood in need'.[3] Such feminine ministrations
were in part effective more for the care and nursing they
offered than for any knowledge of *materia medica*.

With individual Quaker doctors Fox was on excellent
terms, such as Edward Bourne of Worcester, who in turn
delighted in Fox's discourse as they rode away together in
1656, and regarded him as 'of a deep and wonderful
understanding in natural' things as well as spiritual.[4]
Dr Bourne in 1675 sent to Fox as a present a bottle of his
healing water.[5]

Thomas Lower, M.D., was even closer to George Fox,
having become his stepson-in-law as well as sharing his
long Worcester imprisonment, during which he kept a
friendly eye upon his companion. The following passage
written a little later in March 1675 from Swarthmore to
London where George and Margaret Fox were staying

[1] John Aubrey, *Brief Lives* (edited by Andrew Clark, Oxford, 1898),
vol. II, p. 134.
[2] For a description see *A History of the Barclay Family*, Part III, by
H. F. Barclay and A. Wilson-Fox, 1934, pp. 111–14.
[3] *Piety Promoted.*
[4] *F.P.T.* p. 278. On Edward Bourne, 'chemist', see the notes by Norman
Penney, loc. cit. and in II, 384 and III, 336. He is 'the ancient Friend' and
'the Doctor' (for so they called him) mentioned by Samuel Bownas in his
Journal when he visited Worcester about 1700, who so strictly demanded
certificates of travelling Friends. But both the printed *Journal* of Bownas
(1st ed. 1756) as compared with the original MS. in the Swarthmore College
Library and the Ellwood *Journal* of Fox (1694) as compared with the MS.
Journal (Cambridge *Journal*) omit his name. This probably indicates that
Dr Bourne did not remain in the good graces of the Society. Cf. III, p. 232, n. 5.
[5] II, 310.

shows his appreciation of Fox's influence as well as his own reliance on medicine. Children had just been born both to the Lowers and to the Rouses.

> We are all well here. Praised be the Lord. My wife something better since she took some of my pills. Little Margaret a lovely thriving child.
>
> We greatly rejoice to hear of our sister Rous's happy deliverance, and good hour wherein my father visited her, whose company is a blessing to all that see, know and receive him, as he is a blessing to the nations and the joy of his people, the second appearance of him who is blessed for ever.[1]

The belief in Fox's salutary influence thus admitted by a practising physician was doubtless exaggerated by other admirers and forced upon Fox's own attention. He records in his *Journal* in connection with the death of Edward Burrough, who died in 1662/3 after eight months in Newgate Gaol: 'Friends told me that Edward Burrough said, if he had been but an hour with me he should have been well.'[2]

In at least one case the patient appears to have made less of the experience than Fox. I refer to James Claypoole, whose recovery from an attack of the stone while he and Fox were staying at Penn's home is recorded impressively in a dated entry in the 'Book of Miracles'.[3] Knowing that Claypoole's letter-book was extant I eagerly searched to see what statement he would make on that occasion. Writing of Fox's visit in a letter to William Penn in Pennsylvania Claypoole says:

> I believe I shall never forget it. The benefit of his society is highly to be valued. That innocent pure heavenly seasoning savory life that appears always in him as a continual meeting. Thou and

---

[1] Printed in Elisha Bates, *Appeal*, p. 21, from Spence MSS. III, 174. Other references to Mary Lower's ailments including her 'old and hereditary distemper' of headache appear in other letters of her husband. See II, 308 (18th of 12 mo. 1674) and Maria Webb, *Fells* (1896), p. 280; Swarthmore MSS. I, 381 (19th of 2 mo. 1670). There are many semi-medical relations of Fox to his stepchildren and grandchildren in the 'Book of Miracles', e.g. nos. 57 *c*, 57 *d*, 61 *e*, 61–2, 63 *a*, 66 *b*, 66 *c*, 67 *a*. Cf. III, 89, 126, 134.

[2] II, 9. The sentence was omitted by Ellwood.

[3] See no. 75 *b*. Also III, 78.

the Friends in those parts are much engaged to him for his fatherly care for your good and the good of the country and is so glad when he meets with anything of good advice that may be beneficial either inwardly or outwardly. We left him at John Rous's at Islington, where he is I suppose at this time.[1]

This is surely appreciative enough of Fox's spiritual benediction, but there is not a word of his physical influence.

In other respects Fox had little reason to boast of his miracles. Probably not all of them were permanent. In some cases he too may have failed. Further he admitted freely that miracles were wrought by other Friends. In a few instances (at least) they were co-operative in character. Such at least would have been the cure attempted by Howgill and Burrough.[2] Such was the earlier cure of a lame woman in which the silent prayer of Dewsbury, the touch of Farnsworth and the words of Fox apparently co-operated. Though Fox evidently described it in the 'Book of Miracles' (35 *b*), our only full narrative comes from a farewell address of William Dewsbury:

My God hath yet put in my heart to bear a testimony in his name and blessed truth, and I can never forget the day of his great power and blessed appearance, when he first sent me to preach his everlasting gospel and proclaim the day of the Lord to all the people. And also he confirmed the same by signs and wonders, and particularly by a lame woman who went on crutches, where I with my dear brethren George Fox and Richard Farnswarth were cast. And as I cried mightily unto the Lord in secret that he would signally manifest himself at that time amongst us and give witness of his power and presence with us, R.F. in the name of the Lord took her by the hand, and G.F. after spoke to her in the Power of God and bid her stand up, and she did and immediately walked straight, having no need of crutches any more.[3]

---

[1] Manuscript letter-book of James Claypoole at the Historical Society of Pennsylvania, pp. 373–9 (letter to William Penn dated London, 1st of 2 mo. 1683). Cf. *Pennsylvania Magazine of History* (1886), vol. x, p. 271 where, however, this passage is omitted.   [2] See above, p. 12.

[3] *The Faithful Testimony of...William Dewsbery* [1689], unnumbered page near the beginning. Reprinted in Edw. Smith, *Life of William Dewsbury* (1836), pp. 277 f. (Friends' Library, 1838, vol. II, p. 298).

Introduction

The earliest miracle of all recorded by Fox, that at the house of Elizabeth Hooton at Skegby, is also described as though neither Fox nor any other individual had performed it alone,[1] and in a later generalization Fox says: 'She had many meetings at her house where the Lord by his power wrought many miracles to the astonishing of the world and confirming people of the Truth.'[2]

Many of Fox's cures must be treated as the normal control of strong personality over physical or mental illness. 'His commanding presence, his piercing eye and the absolute assurance which his voice gave that he was equal to the occasion were worth a thousand doctors with their lancets.'[3] The *Journal* tells of a stratagem of his enemies at Lancaster in 1652 who brought a distracted man with intent to set him upon Fox to beat him with birch rods, 'but', says the latter, 'I was moved to speak to them in the Lord's mighty power which chained him and them'.[4] There was not merely pious deference on Fox's part in referring his success to the power of the Lord;[5] he felt a kind of fellowship—or shall we say telepathy—with the Divine spirit. In his *Diary* of the voyage to America in 1671 John Hull writes one day:

> Friends were sickish these two or three days, especially John Cartwright who was something feverish, and that evening George Fox was moved to pray for him and felt an intercession for his life.[6]

Even medicine in those days did not sharply differentiate itself from all idea of miracle. Lady Conway (*née* Anne Finch), one of the most famous of Quaker patients in the first generation, no doubt discussed the possibility of miracle with her Quaker friends as it was brought to her

---

[1] See no. 33 *a*.

[2] Manuscript testimony to Elizabeth Hooton. Printed in Emily Manners, *Elizabeth Hooton* (1914), p. 5.

[3] R. M. Jones, *George Fox, an Autobiography* (1904), p. 113.

[4] I, 72 (Ellwood, 1694, p. 92; 1891, I, 143).

[5] See the phrase in nos. 14 *d*, 51 *b*, 60 *b*, 66 *b*, 75 *b*.

[6] II, 179.

attention by others.[1] It would be difficult to say whether the attitude of Francis Mercurius van Helmont, who long attended this afflicted but brilliant lady, should be compared with modern medicine or with magic. A Quaker himself, and the son of a leading medical authority, he was doubtless somewhat in the position of family doctor for the family at Ragley Hall from 1670 to her death in 1678/9. More miraculous were the claims of Valentine Greatrakes, the touch doctor. At the invitation of Lord Conway he came over from Ireland to try his skill on the noble patient in 1665. Upon her ailment of chronic headache he had no effect, but in hundreds of other cases he appeared to be successful, and first at Ragley and later in London he secured the endorsement of authorities of all kinds, political, scientific and religious, who accepted his cures as genuine. But within a year, either his energy or his effectiveness or his reputation waned, he returned to Ireland and passed many years there in obscurity until his death.[2]

Outside of Quaker circles genuine miracles would not be denied by Fox. In Amsterdam in 1677 he met 'a woman at the meeting who had gone 14 years on her hands and her knees and through the wonderful hand and arm of the Lord was this year restored'.[3] A fuller account of this woman, Jeske Claes, wife of Rinck Abbis, boatman on the Prince's Island in Amsterdam harbour, is

---

[1] See Robert Gell's letter, mentioned above, p. 2.

[2] For Greatrakes and Lord and Lady Conway, see *The Friend* (Philadelphia, 1850), vol. XXIII, pp. 212, 219, 228. The following pamphlets are of interest, especially for the detailed cases listed much as in Fox's 'Book of Miracles', with witnesses. (The witnesses include frequently Albertus Otto Faber, M.D. & Medicus Regius Exercitus Suecici' who at the time was pretty much of a Quaker. See *J.F.H.S.* (1935), vol. XXXII, pp. 54 ff.) Henry Stubbe, *The Miraculous Conformist* (Oxford, 1666); David Lloyd, *Wonders no Miracles* (1666); *A Brief Account of Mr. Valentine Greatrak's,...Written by himself in a letter addressed to the Honourable Robert Boyle, Esq.* (1666). Marjorie Nicolson, *Conway Letters* (1930) should be consulted both for Greatrakes (ch. v) and van Helmont (ch. VI). A visit between 'V. Gratricks' and William Penn in Ireland on 28 April 1670 is mentioned by the latter in his Journal. See *Pennsylvania Magazine* (1916), vol. XL, p. 76.

[3] III, 252, under date of 10th of 8 mo. Omitted by Ellwood.

available.[1] There is, however, no evidence that she was a Friend.

On the other hand Fox would be as sceptical as any member of the English Church of some of the miracles claimed either by other sectaries or by Roman Catholics. The latter he openly challenged in Ireland, to test the alleged miracle of the Mass.[2]

One of the few accounts preserved of controversy between Quakers and Roman Catholics is that of Katharine Evans and Sarah Cheevers, while prisoners of the Inquisition in the Island of Malta from 1659 to 1662. Katharine Evans relates that the inquisitors on one occasion told them that 'we [the Quakers] were but few, and had been but a little while, and they [the Catholics] were many countries, and had stood many hundred years, and wrought many miracles, and we had none. We said, we had thousands at our meetings, but none of us dare speak a word, but as they are eternally moved of the Lord; and we had miracles; the blind receive their sight, the deaf do hear, and the dumb do speak, the poor do receive the gospel, the lame

---

[1] Apparently a Dutch account was printed in 1677 at Amsterdam, for English translations in MS. are to be found in the Colchester MSS. (no. 67) and in the Philadelphia Yearly Meeting Archives (R.S. 198). The former, like all the collection, is from the papers of Steven Crisp. See C. Fell Smith, *Steven Crisp and his Correspondents, 1657–1692*, p. 35. The latter is derived from its being 'a copy taken from one in the hands of John Churchman who brought it from Chelmsford'. The cure is dated October 1676, a year before. See Wm. I. Hull, *William Penn and the Dutch Quaker Migration* (1935), p. 92, who gives the English text but mentions no Dutch title, nor do I find any in the well-known Dutch pamphlet catalogues of Knuttel, Meulman, Muller or Tiele. But L. A. O. Petit, *Bibliotheek van Nederlandsche Pamfletten* (Hague, 1884), vol. II, mentions two pieces at the Bibliotheca Thysiana in Leiden which evidently deal with the event, nos. 4337 and 4338 dated in 1676 at Alkmaar and Rotterdam respectively.

[2] II, 138. The nature of this challenge may be learned from 'A Challenge to the Papists', dated Ireland, the 19th of 3 mo. 1669, and signed by Fox and his companions (Lancaster, Stubbs and Briggs). It was printed the same year in the pamphlet, *A Few Words to all Such whether Papists or Protestants*, pp. 11 f. In 1688 Fox attacked a different miraculous claim of the Roman Catholics in his pamphlet, *Concerning the Apostate Christians that think to do Miracles by Dead Mens Bones*, etc. (See pp. 3 f.)

do walk, and the dead are raised'.[1] On another occasion she quotes a Friar as arguing similarly that we [the Quakers] were but few and risen up but late, and they [the Catholics] were many and had stood 1400 years, and God was a liar if they had not the true faith, for he had confirmed it to them by a thousand miracles.[2]

All these concrete experiences and contacts made Fox neither credulous nor incredulous but discriminating, and they restrained him in referring to his own miracles. Other Friends may have been more cautious in making claims. We know more explicitly their theological views about the relation of Truth to contemporary miracle. Probably Fox shared or even inherited such views as we have quoted from Saltmarsh or Barclay or Penington. He was, however, independent, 'an original, being no man's copy', and in spite of all self-criticism and realized danger of exaggeration he felt clearly that the miracles that surrounded his life and the beginnings of the Quaker movement were too numerous and too significant to be ignored. A collection of these was worth making to have upon record.

THE LOST BOOK—RECOVERY AND CONTENTS

Although the 'Book of Miracles' is lost, I have been able to reconstruct a considerable amount of its contents in a manner which is so unusual that it must be described. *The Annual Catalogue of George Fox's Papers* made in 1694 to 1698 and published in part in 1939 was accompanied in

---

[1] *This is a Short Relation of some of the Cruel Sufferings (for the Truth's Sake) of Katharine Evans and Sarah Chevers* (London, 1662), p. 9. The revised edition, *A Brief History of the Voyage of Katharine Evans and Sarah Cheevers* (London, 1715), adds at the end of the passage above quoted the word 'mystically' (p. 18). This accords with the attitude of the later Quaker editors (see p. 27) and may accord with the intent of the original account. It is of interest that that original was preserved and published by Daniel Baker, whose literal cure of lameness was told in Fox's 'Book of Miracles' (see below, nos. 55 *b*, 65 *a–b*). For the appropriation by Friends of the words of Jesus' reply to John the Baptist (Matt. xi. 5; Luke vii. 22) compare above, p. 21, below, p. 91.

[2] Ibid. (1662), p. 16; (1715), p. 39.

the same volume by an alphabetical index dated 1695. Each key word is entered in its alphabetical place, and under it, according to the manner of the time, the first and last words of the passage containing it and a reference to the collection and page in Fox's writings in which the cataloguer found it. These collections were abbreviated by one or more letters like the signatures in a book, viz. A, a, Aa or aa, and there is a key to the collections. This key gives opposite the symbol O (the capitalized vowel—not the number zero) the explanation: 'Gff's miracles, fol. bound mst.'[1] This suggests that when one reads in the index on p. 733:

Foster)

Mary Foster one of her...restored to health	15	O
Mary Foster who lives in L...to the praise of the Lord.	63	O

one may infer that on p. 15 of the 'Book of Miracles' was one narrative which began and ended with the words given on the first line, and on p. 63 another narrative about the same person using the words of the second line. Although the Catalogue proper ignored this collection,[2] the index contains about 350 references to it. By picking out from the index with its entries (some 15,000 in number) those with the symbol O, one could get an outline of the contents of the whole book. But since each paragraph was indexed usually under more than one word, by arranging them in order, it was possible to reduce the total items and increase the information about each. Thus the same two citations above were indexed under 'sick' also. Indexed under 'woman', under 'pain' and under 'head' we find this entry:

A woman had a great pain in her head...her pain went away.	26	O

[1] In the index itself occurs this obscure entry: 'Gff's book of miracles marked with the letter O min. p. 323.' I suppose p. 323 in a book of minutes is meant, but the reference does not fit any minute books known to me.   [2] For a single exception see note to no. 17.

VI. Part of page 734 of the Manuscript Index to Annual Catalogue of George Fox showing entries from the 'Book of Miracles', pages 31, 73, 75

Indexed under 'Myers' and under 'arm' we find the following:

In Westmorland in a great m...heard it and saw it.   53   O

Obviously this incident had to do with a person named Myers and an affected arm. In this case it is possible to identify the event with one known to us elsewhere: the cure of Richard Myers' arm by George Fox at Arnside in Westmorland in 1653. There are several more of these brief entries that can be identified with events told in Fox's *Journal*.

Below is given the result of the combining of the several index entries. The page number is retained, but I have added a letter (*a*, *b*, *c*, etc.) to differentiate items on the same page. When, as in the instance just mentioned, there is a parallel account in Fox's *Journal* of what is obviously the same event, that is added in smaller type. In six cases the full text of the item is extant. This is proved by the exact agreement of each with the first and the last words as given in the index. These are printed in the same type throughout, the square brackets indicating what was between the first and last words cited in the index. To mark each of the words under which each item was indexed I have used an asterisk, but I have not indicated the number of the page in the MS. index from which each citation is derived.

In all, 171 episodes were related. They began on p. 7, and ended on p. 79. The preceding pages may have contained an introduction, but evidently much of the book was blank since 200 pages later are three apparently unrelated entries:

Dear mother, The two posts last...loving daughter,
Isabel Yeamans.*   276   O

Friends, while you do keep to the witness*...things
of God.   285   O

Upon the 14. 11 mo. 79...vision*...at night like a
confusion.   285   O

Also in the book proper occurs some less homogeneous material—not quite unmiraculous, but belonging rather to the other categories of Fox's collections. Two and probably four instances of persecutors being foiled or punished were recorded on pp. 73–5 (cf. no. 61 *d*), and there was a vision or two. I am not sure that what was contained in nos. 31 *c* and 32 *a* was really relevant. For the rest, as the entries themselves show, the material was largely uniform in character. In the incomplete as in the complete entries the following motifs frequently appeared: a statement of the patient's ailment, Fox's intervention, the immediacy and permanence of the improvement, the thanksgiving to God, the wonder of the spectators.[1] The faith of the patient or the power of God is also noted.[2] More than a dozen have either the year or a fuller date at the beginning or end, ranging from 1650 to 1685. These limits must be extended in either direction to accommodate nos. 32 *b* and 77 *a* respectively. The former belongs to 1649, the latter apparently to 1689. Some of the other items can be dated more or less either by parallel accounts or by other evidence.

There were in many cases references to persons or places by name. But the place-name is often only the county, and many other accounts even if the text had been fully preserved would not have proved quite as circumstantial.

Of the named persons I have been fortunate in being able to identify the greater number. Most of them were Friends, some of them well-known Friends. For those who are mentioned in Penney's editions of Fox's major and minor journals I have been satisfied to refer simply to his biographical notes, adding any information I have which was not apparently known to him. The reader of the present

---

[1] I need scarcely remind the reader that such items are regular in the miracle stories of all religions. The references to the doctors (nos. 8, 50 *a*) are also typical, as are those to the disuse of crutches (nos. 60 *a*, 65 *b*; cf. no. 14 *c*), and to the quantity of miracles unrecorded (nos. 52 *d*, 54–5).

[2] Nos. 10 *a*, 37 *d*, 42 *a–b*, 56 *f*, 61–2, 62 *b*.

volume who wishes biographical identifications should have the other three volumes by him.

In many cases Fox himself did not know or did not remember the names. Evidently his meetings with the afflicted persons were often casual or accidental. It must be assumed that in many cases they were not and never became Friends. Probably a certain amount of public fame as a healer accompanied Fox on his travels and brought strangers to him.

At least two of the persons were so well known that their illnesses became a matter of public concern. They were Elizabeth Claypole, favourite daughter of Oliver Cromwell, who died 6 August 1658, and the young Duke of Gloucester, son of Prince George and Princess (later Queen) Anne, and heir-apparent, who was born in 1689. Contemporary records reflect the widespread interest in both of these noble invalids, and the efforts made to suggest remedies. For example, just before Lady Claypole's death, her sister, Lady Frances Rich, received from Christian Cavendish, Countess Dowager of Devonshire, a letter, which for its lay outlook on medicine and miracle is worth quoting in part:

I bear a very great part of your trouble and grief at this time for your most worthy sister. My lady's fits being so terrible, and her weakness increasing, I thought it fit to offer to your consideration a remedy that I had recommended to me when I was in my great extremity winter was twelvemonth. It is called the universal cure, or quintessence of gold; the gentleman that makes it lives in Shropshire and I have heard that the medicine has done miraculous cures, and that to very young children, the remedy being very safe.... I presume not to offer this as a fit cure for my lady further than as the physicians shall approve of it. I know most of them look upon these remedies as irregular and extravagant. Yet in great extremities they have been consenting, when other medicines have not prevailed.[1]

The death of 'the pretty Duke of Gloucester', leading as it did to the ultimate Protestant succession of the House of

---

[1] *Report on the MSS. of Mrs. Frankland-Russell Astley of Chequers Court, Bucks* (Historical Manuscripts Commission (1900), vol. LII) p. 23.

Hanover, was recognized by William Penn when he first heard it in Philadelphia as likely to 'cause thoughts and fresh measures at home among the grandees'.[1]

In such a large collection of detached items some repetition may well have occurred by accident. Thus I suspect no. 21 *a* is a doublet of no. 70 *a*, while perhaps nos. 55 *b*, 60 *a* and 65 *b* are three references to the same recovery.

Some consisted of letters—from Margaret Greenway (no. 12 *b*), Brian Sixmith (no. 20), Charles Lloyd (no. 22 *d*), Clare Hartas (no. 27 *b*) and others (no. 61–2). There were probably signed testimonies of Mary Elson and Agnes Pool (nos. 64 *a*, 64 *b*). The account of John Banks was written by him in the first person (no. 62 *a*). Fox's own accounts were written some in the first person and some in the third. In some cases the two were mixed or imperfectly edited into uniformity (nos. 10 *a*, 11 *b*, 12 *a*). For the narratives just referred to we have evidence that they were originally written by Fox in his own hand.

From what has been said it is clear that the book was a compilation of independent units. Its order was not systematic, but occasionally its units followed each other by some natural association of ideas—the same person, the same kind of ailment, the same year, or even actual sequence in fact suggesting what should follow. Adjacent paragraphs sometimes resembled each other in the manner of telling, e.g. 'to this day' at the end of nos. 69 *a* and 69 *b*, 'etc.' at the end of nos. 61 *a*, 61 *b*, 61 *c* and 61 *d*.

Tantalizingly incomplete as most of the entries are, they are nevertheless surprisingly informative. The indexer fortunately listed most of them under the word which referred to the ailment and thus preserved some idea of the scope of medical phenomena involved, though we could desire more explicit symptoms in place of phrases like 'sick' (45 times), or 'weak', or 'not well', or 'dying'. The patients were women perhaps more often than men, and

---

[1] Letter to James Logan, 1 September 1700, in *Memoirs of the Historical Society of Pennsylvania* (1870), vol. IX, p. 19.

there were several children. Ague and fever is a frequent combination. There are several instances each of King's evil, ulcers and small-pox. Mental diseases are represented by several persons called 'distracted' or 'possessed' or 'moping' or 'star-gazing'. Evidently not all the incidents referred to successful cures. Certainly some (nos. 11 *b*, 66 *b*) and probably others dealt with cases that ended fatally. Probably some instances are of cures reported to Fox (no. 10 *a*). Beside those in which Fox was present were others in which he exercised his influence from a distance by letter (no. 17)[1] or messenger (no. 8).

Of special interest to modern readers are the materials indicating the extent to which the cures of Fox were of mental ailments. Of the total list of cures one can no longer say in the light of the fuller evidence, as was said half a century ago, 'at its utmost the list is a short one',[2] nor of the larger number of cures indicated but not fully preserved from the 'Book of Miracles' is the proportion of mental cases as high as in the *Journal* where of twelve cases 'six were distracted, moping or mentally-disturbed people'.[3] The vocabulary for mental illness was different in the seventeenth century from our own, as was the vocabulary of the first-century Gospels, and probably at no period could a sharp line of cleavage be drawn between mental and physical. Of over 150 cases in the 'Book of Miracles', fourteen are indexed under 'distracted', two (probably a doublet) under 'moping' and one each under 'possessed' and 'troubled'. The latter term probably, and certainly 'in trouble' and 'stargazing', were terms then for mental phenomena and so sometimes the very frequent and vague word 'sick', under which forty-five paragraphs in the 'Book of Miracles' are listed. Similarly, of over twenty persons in

---

[1] The letter dated 1658 is published by Ellwood (1694), pp. 189 f. Fox speaks of its service in settling the minds of other distracted persons in England and Ireland. Probably a similar purpose was intended by a letter which he wrote in 1653 'to one who was weak, whom the Lord's power raised up'. (*Annual Catalogue*, 19, 14 A.)

[2] F. S. Turner, *The Quakers* (1889), p. 126.

[3] H. E. Collier, *Friends' Quarterly Examiner* (1944), vol. LXXVIII, p. 287.

Introduction

or about London mentioned in the *Itinerary Journal* (1683–
90), as visited by George Fox because they were 'sick' or
'not well', two are described as 'not well in mind' or
'muddled in mind' respectively.[1]

More systematic interest or provision for the insane,
such as led to the founding of the York Retreat in 1796,
and later of the Friends' asylums in Frankford near
Philadelphia and at Asfûriyeh in Syria,[2] as well as to the
Mental Health Foundation in 1945, was not wanting in the
early Quakers. In one of his epistles Fox urged 'Friends to
have and provide a house for them that be distempered,
and not to go to the world'.[3] This probably suggested the
instructions sent down from the Six Weeks Meeting, and
now preserved among the papers of Ratcliff Monthly
Meeting dated 11th of 5 mo. 1671:

That Friends do seek some place convenient in or about the City
wherein they may put any person that may be distracted or
troubled in mind, that so they may not be put amongst the
world's people or run about the streets.[4]

Soon after apparently a house for 'distempered and dis-
composed persons' was opened in London. In America, as
early as 1751, in consequence of a concern of Philadelphia

[1] III, 90 and 171. See notes to nos. 46 and 48, p. 128. Other cases of
affliction mentioned in early Quaker sources include a lunatic Friend who
cut his own throat (III, 349) and a Virginia school-teacher who intermittently
fell into distraction of mind so as to destroy his clothes and do other
destructive things (*Friend* (Philadelphia, 1897), vol. LXXI, p. 169).

[2] Samuel Tuke, *Description of the Retreat* (1813); Harold C. Hunt, *A
Retired Habitation* (1932); L. A. G. Strong, *Light through the Cloud* (1946);
Account of the Rise and Progress of the Asylum Proposed near Philadelphia
(1814); *Friends' Asylum for the Insane 1813–1913* (1913); T. Waldmeier,
Autobiography, revision of 1925, edited by Stephen Hobhouse, Part v, The
Lebanon Hospital for the Insane.

[3] *Epistles* (1698), p. 287. This epistle (no. 264) is dated in 1669 and the
first part of it was widely circulated in manuscript. The printed epistle is
composite and the passage may have been written by Fox later.

[4] Isaac Sharp, *The Friend* (London, 1901), vol. XLI, p. 714. Bedford
Pierce, 'The Treatment of the Insane, a Survey of the Work of Friends
in England and America', *Friends' Quarterly Examiner* (1902), vol. XXXVI,
pp. 73 f. Cf. ibid. (1938), vol. LXXII, p. 80.

Monthly Meeting, a portion of the Pennsylvania Hospital was set apart for the treatment of persons 'distemper'd in mind, and deprived of their rational faculties'. The York Retreat was partly the result of the death of a member of Friends in 1791 in York asylum, under circumstances which roused suspicions of the kind of treatment she had received. Thus, without tracing it further, we can see that the Quaker concern was partly for the separation of Friends from non-Friends, partly the separation of the insane from the mentally well, and partly the concern for wiser special treatment of those afflicted.[1]

CONTEMPORARY PUBLICATIONS OF MIRACLES

If Fox's executors had decided to publish the 'Book of Miracles' it would not have stood unique among the printed materials of the time. I proceed, therefore, with reference to some nearly contemporary collections, quoting some examples that can be compared with the method of presentation used by Fox.

There was considerable literature about miracles at the end of the seventeenth century in England. Beside the providences and judgements which are mentioned elsewhere, there were portents in nature. The prolific author R.B. had published in 1685 the second edition of his work, *The Surprizing Miracles of Nature and Art*, a work which William Penn recommended for a high-born young Quaker to read.[2] More akin to the incidents in Quaker journals is the publication of the escapes of travellers from danger, as in the section on 'Admirable Deliverances from Imminent Dangers and Deplorable Distresses at Sea and Land' in a book by the same R.B.[3] An earlier work was devoted

---

[1] Beside the material mentioned in the earlier notes, see on Friends' care of the insane, A. Jorns, op. cit. pp. 152–61.

[2] S. F. Locker Lampson, *A Quaker Post-Bag* (1910), p. 6.

[3] *Wonderful Prodigies of Judgment and Mercy discovered in above Three Hundred Memorable Histories* (1685), pp. 181–214. No. 12 in this series is a variant of the story in Chalkley's *Journal* mentioned in J. G. Whittier's *Snowbound*. A ship of New England going from Boston was delayed and became so short of food that lots were taken deciding upon the first person

entirely to *Remarkable Sea Deliverances*; and a selection of 'Wonderful Sea Deliverances' constitutes the first chapter in the sixth book of Cotton Mather's *Magnalia Christi Americana*. Mention has already been made of experiences of this sort among early Friends.

Of dangers upon land the experiences of travellers among the American Indians are among the most conspicuous. Both of these motifs appear in Fox's *Journals* and other Quaker literature. They are combined a few years after Fox's death in the harrowing tale of shipwreck off Florida of Robert Barrow and his companions.[1] There was plenty of material on such escapes in Quaker experience, and a collection of them would have suited contemporary taste in reading and publication. It would also make very interesting reading to-day. Along with its thoroughly edifying religious feature of miracle and Providence, it would satisfy the very natural and secular human craving for excitement and adventure. It appears, however, to have played a very small part in Fox's 'Book of Miracles' That dealt almost entirely with disease and health. To literature of miraculous cures we accordingly turn for analogies.

As parallels for style of presentation we may compare first the bills of contemporary physicians and quacks of which many examples have come down to us from the period of Fox's activity. Here is part of an account of cures 'lately performed on persons of quality' by Cornelius a Tilbourn, 'sworn Chyrurgeon to King Charles II':

> Sir Richard Greeneway, troubled with the stone was speedily cured by me. John Owen, Esquire, who so honourably served his late Majesty in the Dutch engagements and had five or six ulcerated holes in his legs, occasioned by splinters, and at first but ill

to be killed and eaten by his companions. First a fish and then a large bird offered themselves, and kept the travellers alive until they were relieved by another vessel.

[1] Jonathan Dickinson, *God's Protecting Providence* (Philadelphia, 1699), and many later editions. See *Bulletin of Friends' Historical Association* (1935), vol. xxiv, pp. 84 ff. and the definitive edition by E. W. and C. M. Andrews, New Haven, 1945.

patched up: in less than six weeks I made him sound and well. The lady Ann Seymoure, that had a lameness in her limbs, that she was forced to keep her bed for four years, was cured by me in seven weeks time, and I also cured a cancerated lip of Sir John Andrews at St James's. Mr Christopher Shelly hard by Cupid's Bridge in Lambeth, was brought to me in a chair, deprived of all his limbs, uncapable of moving hand or foot was (by the blessing of God) perfectly cured by me, to the admiration of all.[1]

Albertus Otto Faber, Royal Physician of the Swedish Army, and later for Charles II in England, should probably be regarded also as a member of the Society of Friends at least for a time.[2] In 1663 he published under the king's protection at London a four-page pamphlet entitled *A Relation of some notable Cures accounted incurable*. These are not really miracles but rather advertisements reporting his successful use of certain remedies as *Ens primum Acidularum Germaniae* and *Oleum de Lapide Butleri*, or discussing the treatment of certain diseases.

Reference was made above to the cures of Valentine Greatrakes. No effort apparently was made by him to record individual cures until a request for such evidence was made by Robert Boyle, the noted English scientist, upon which a collection of about fifty records were secured in writing signed and witnessed which were printed at the close of a pamphlet already cited.[3] The items are either in the form of letters or are called 'certificates' or 'testimonies'. The last term and the attest of witnesses remind us of some items in Fox's 'Book of Miracles'. They are all dated within the short space of March, April and May 1666. The diseases—usually treated by stroking—include nearly all

---

[1] Quoted in C. J. S. Thompson, *The Quacks of Old London* (1928), pp. 87 f.

[2] His medical and other writings are duly listed in Joseph Smith's *Descriptive Catalogue of Friends' Books*. Accounts of him are given by John L. Nickalls in *J.F.H.S.* (1935), vol. XXXII, pp. 54–7, and more fully by Harriet Sampson, 'Dr Faber and his Celebrated Cordial' in *Isis* (1943), vol. XXXIV, pp. 472–96.

[3] *A Brief Account of Mr Valentine Greatrak's* (1666), pp. 43–94.

specific ailments mentioned in Fox's 'Book of Miracles'
A few examples are quoted below:

Mr. *Boyle's,* and Dr. *Faireclough's* Testimony.

Robert Furnace a Mettleman in *Clarkenwell* Parish lame for
8 years, had been thrice in St. *Bartholomews* Hospital, for eleven
weeks at one time, and nine or ten weeks for a second time, and for
a month the last time, without benefit, being in great pain in
his hips and thighs, legs and feet, was stroked by Mr. *Greatrak's,*
April 3. 1666. and found present ease in his hip upon the first
touch of Mr. *Greatrak's* hand, wherewith the said *Furnace's* pain
was driven downward from place to place without much grievance,
until it came to his foot, but when the pain was only in his foot, it
was then most intollerable in it, which being gently stroked, he was
quite freed from all pain, and walked without his Crutches, which
he could not have done for seven years before. Attested by
himself this sixth day of *April* 1666.

Robert Furnace.

In presence of
  Ro. Boyle.
  Ja. Faireclough M.D.[1]

Dr. Faireclough's *and Dr.* Faber's *Testimony. April* 19. 1666.

Sarah Tuffly, Servant to Mr. *John Pryde* at the *Red Cross* nigh
Essex-gate in the *Strand,* troubled with a violent Head-ach every
day more or less for 7 years; upon Mr. *Greatrak's* stroking her head
she fell a belching, which continued for two hours and upwards, he
now and then applying his hand to her breast, *&c.* whereupon she
was freed from all pains, though her tongue was at times as cold as
lead, during this process; and now declares her self more free from
any manner of pain then she has been these 9 years.

Sarah Tuffly.

Before Us,
  Tho. Kenian Gent.
  Alb. Otto Faber Med.
  J. Faireclough M.D.
  W. Smith Chir.[2]

---

[1] *A Brief Account of Mr Valentine Greatrak's, and Divers of the Strange
Cures By him lately Performed* (London, 1666), pp. 48–9.
[2] Ibid. p. 76.

Introduction

Dr. Cudworth's *Certificate*.

SIR,

I Can certifie you that the tumours in my little Son *Charles* his breast are very happily cured by *Mr. Greatrak's*, who opened the same, and let out the corrupt matter, and since the sores are healed, and the wounds dryed up.

April 18. 1666   *R. Cudworth*, D.D.[1]

A collection of miracles is included by the famous Henry More in his addition to Joseph Glanvill's *Saducismus Triumphatus*. They are largely in the realm of Spiritualism, but they include for example 'the miraculous cure of Jesch Claes' as taken by a Dutch merchant from her own mouth, and fortified by the Dutch printed narrative already mentioned, 'which Monsieur van Helmont brought over with him to my Lady Conway, who, having inquired upon the spot when he was there at Amsterdam, though of a genius not at all credulous of such relations, found the thing to be really true. As also Philipus Limbergius in a letter to Dr H. More sent his testimony touching the party cured, that she was always reputed a very honest good woman, and that he believed there was no fraud at all in the business'.[2] It should be recalled that Francis Mercurius van Helmont as well as Lady Conway were Friends. The latter is mentioned more than once in More's treatise.

No type of miracle enjoyed more widespread popularity and credence than the cure of scrofula by the touch of kings. This belief was at its height during Fox's lifetime, as Macaulay describes it in his *History of England*.[3] As Fox himself testifies, it was commonly known as the King's evil. The monarch to cure the patient touched him with his hands and gave a gold piece (sometimes hung upon a ribbon) as a charm to confirm and continue the cure. In 1684 John Browne, Chirurgeon in Ordinary to his Majesty, Charles II, wrote an extensive treatise on the subject, from

[1] Ibid. p. 60.   [2] 3rd ed. 1689, pp. 427 f.
[3] Ed. of 1855, vol. III, pp. 478–80.

75

the viewpoint both of medical diagnosis and of miraculous cure.[1] The last section, called 'Charisma Basilicon', includes in the appendix the numbers touched by the above-named monarch each year from 1660 to 1682. Evidently they add up to above 90,000 persons during his whole reign. Some fifty 'Several Examples of Miraculous Cure Performed by his Majesties Sacred Touch' occupy the seventy pages of his chapter x. Some of them are told on the author's own authority, some on evidence he quotes. In some cases he includes, like Fox, the letters of his informants addressed to himself. By way of illustration, I quote three items in which two of the patients are described as having been Quakers either before they were cured, or at some later date. The third was a sectary, often confused with Friends,[2] though of a rather more political type.

Woman Quaker of Guilford

There was a Woman Quaker which lived at *Guilford* in *Surry*, who being so perfectly blind, that she was rob'd of all light and sight: She coming to *Hampton-Court*, where our late King was then a Prisoner, to be touch'd by His Sacred Majesty; so soon as she received the same, or within less than an hour after the reception thereof, she went down to the Kings kitchin, and did there tell the number of Spits which were turning upon the Range, and did there fall down upon her knees, praying to God to forgive her for those evil thoughts she formerly had of her good King, by whom she had receiv'd this great Blessing. Mr. *John Stephens* of the Kings Back-stairs, was an eye-witness of every part hereof, he being then at the Operation, and afterwards seeing her in the Kitchin: At this time the King did only put over her Neck a Silver Two pence, strung in a white Silk Ribband; and this may prove, that other Metal used and imployed by the Sacred Hand, does the

---

[1] For later treatises see William Beckett, *A Free and Impartial Enquiry into...Touching for the Cure of the King's Evil* (1722); Raymond Crawfurd, *The King's Evil* (1911); Marc Bloch, *Les rois thaumaturges* (1924). The last of these extends to 542 pages and contains a full bibliography.

[2] A copy of Evans' *Voice from Heaven to the Common Wealth of England* (1653) is listed in *Bibliotheca Furliana* (Rotterdam, 1714), among Quaker books. In another copy in my possession 'Quaker' has been written in an early hand after his name on the title-page. On Evans see *D.N.B.*

same as Gold. All People which did here come to be touch'd had only Silver given to them, and yet most of them known to be cured; and such as fail'd thereof, hapned chiefly from their unbelief and incredulity. Mr. *Henry Ewer*, four years of age, was brought by the former Mr. *Stephens* to be touch'd by His late Sacred Majesty at *Hampton-Court* at the same time; his Eyes being so sore and ill-affected, that he could not look upon any Fire, or behold the light of the Sun or Moon, they were so weak and troublesom to him: within a Month or six Weeks after his being healed by the King, he was seen perfectly discharged from his pain, and recovered to admiration, and lived many years free from all trouble: Both these Mr. *Stephens* is ready to maintain, if at any time he may be questioned about the same.[1]

Gunsmith in Winchester

Mr. *John Stephens* of His Majesties Back-stairs, acquaints me of a Gun-Smith in *Winchester*, who being a Quaker, and very much troubled with the *Evil* in his Neck, he coming to him to desire the procuring him a Ticket, in order to his being healed by the King: No sooner had this Quaker this Ticket given him, but he tells Mr. *Stephens* his Faith was so small, that he did not believe the Kings Touch could much help him, or that there was any Power or Virtue therein, but resolved notwithstanding to make use of his Favor. This Quaker no sooner sees the King, but his Spirits immediately raised to a higher degree of Faith, and begot a greater belief in him, telling Mr. *Stephens* that his mind was quite altered, and he was certain His Majesty would heal him. This Quaker, within less than 48 hours after his being Touch'd, was very much amended, and before he could get home, was wholly discharged from his Swellings in his Neck: and as a publick acknowledgment to Almighty God for his great Cure, he went to the Cathedral Church at *Winchester* the first Sunday following, to pay his publick Thanks: And when he heard the King prayed for, he was taken notice of being more concern'd than at any other part of the Prayers, by lifting up his Hands as a greater and more sincere acknowledgment of the extraordinary Blessing he lately received, and is and hath ever since remained a true Son of the Church.[2]

[1] John Browne, *Adenochoiradelogia* (London, 1684), bk. III, pp. 141–2.
[2] John Browne, op. cit. pp. 172–3.

Introduction

Arise Evans

The same Mr. *Butler* tells me, that within a small time after our Kings coming into *England, Elias Ashmole* Esq; Comptroler of the Excise, acquainted him with this following Observation, of one Arrice Evans, who then went generally by the name of *Evans the Prophet*, who being troubled with a very despicable and blasted Face, so that it was not only nauseous to view, but very fetid of smell, he coming to Mr. *Ashmole* to request the favour of his getting him toucht by His Majesty for the same, he utterly refused it, not thinking him a fit person to approach His Majesties Presence; and being stript of all hope or advantage from him, as also from many others which he had endeavoured to procure: He being utterly denyed the attaining the favour of the Kings Presence by any interest of Friends, at last resolves with himself (with an assured Faith, that if His Majesty did but touch him he should speedily recover) to attend the Kings coming by him in the usual Walks he takes in St. *James's Park*; the King at length coming that way, his Face being covered with a Red Cloath, the which he lifted up till he saw the King near him, which he afterwards letting fall down, cries out, *I am 'Rise Evans*. The King coming nearer him with his Attendants which waited on Him, some of them told His Majesty that he was His Majesties Prophet; the King coming at him, he kneels down, and cries, *God bless Your Majesty*: The Good King gives him His Hand to Kiss, and he rubbing his ulcerated and scabbed Nose therewith, which was plentifully stockt with purulent and fetid matter: within two days after his reception of His Majesties sacred favour, the abovesaid Mr. *Ashmole* saw this *Evans* cured, and his ulcered Nose dryed up and healed. This Mr. *Butler* tells me he had it from Mr. *Ashmole's* own mouth.[1]

Such royal cures had political quite as much as religious implications. This is obviously the case with Arise Evans, who had predicted the King's return. It is clearly shown when the cures are attributed to claimants or pretenders to the throne. Thus a four-page broadside entitled *A Choice Collection of Wonderful Miracles, Ghosts and Visions*[2] has as its obvious motive the relation of cures of the King's evil

[1] John Browne, op. cit. pp. 162–4.

[2] Printed for Benjamin Harris (London, 1681). A copy is in the Harvard College Library.

wrought by the touch of the Duke of Monmouth and even of his sister Mrs F.[1] Yet the method of narration is typical of all miracle stories. Elizabeth Parcet, aged 20 years, of Crewkerne, Somerset, had tried all the chirurgeons, and even travelled ten or eleven miles to a seventh son,[2] but all in vain. Jonathan Trott, aged about 19 years, of London, was suffering from a complaint finally diagnosed by Dr Lower,[3] Dr Mishel, etc., as King's evil. It was revealed to each of them to go to the royal benefactor. The second patient did not even know the Duke had a sister. But in both cases a cure was effected.

A better-known author, though not a better-known book, may be cited: Cotton Mather's *Things for a Distress'd People to Think Upon.* Mather's thesis is that just as 'miracles were continued in the Church of God for two or three hundred years together even until the antichristian apostasy was come on to some extremity', so 'when that apostasy is over, 'tis possible there may be a return to proper miracles, those powers of the world to come'. He warns that the examples he gives are perhaps only 'symbolical representations and exhibitions of the things which the Lord is going to do for his people' and that the reader is not sinfully to expect miracles,[4] especially not to encourage himself in vain expectation of miracles to relieve his particular affliction; but he gives in full no less than seven definite cases.[5] Though his book was printed in Boston in 1696, the stories pertain mostly to London and to the years 1693 to 1694. Evidently most of them were derived by Mather from a single letter of the Reverend John Howe. The patients had recovered in most cases as a result of reading the stories of cure in the Gospels. Their names and dates are mostly given in detail. The complaints

---

[1] Mary, half-sister to James Scott, Duke of Monmouth, and wife of William Fanshawe.

[2] Second only to the currency of the belief in the efficacy of the royal touch was the tradition that scrofula could be cured by a seventh son.

[3] This Dr Lower is probably Dr Richard Lower, physician to Charles II, and brother to Thomas Lower, the Quaker and son-in-law of George Fox.

[4] Pp. 36 f.　　　　　　　　　　[5] Pp. 77–86.

included palsy, King's evil, fistula, leprosy and consumption (phthisis). The following is selected partly because like one item in Fox's 'Book of Miracles' it deals with a blackamoor, and partly because it is evidently reproduced in the wording of Howe's letter:

A fourth [miracle] I have late certain knowledge of (but the thing was done six years ago) of a Blackamoor youth, servant unto a religious Baronet. He lately dining at my house assured me that his servant having a great aversion to Christianity and refusing instruction was struck with universal pains in all his limbs which continued upon him a year and a half, like rheumatical, but relieved by none of the apt usual means, that are wont to give relief in such cases. At length in his torments which were great he grew serious, instructible, penitent; and by the frequent endeavours of the parochial minister (a good man, known to me) brought to an understanding acknowledgement of Christ; upon which Baptism being promised unto him he consented, but pressed to be carried unto the assembly that he might own Christ publicly; upon the doing whereof he was immediately cured, and hath continued well ever since.[1]

Another of Mather's examples had already received considerable attention in print, and was doubtless derived from that source by him. On 26 November 1693, Mary Maillard, a French Protestant refugee in London, aged 13 years, was cured from a severe lameness and deformity which she had had almost since she was born. The details were set forth in 1694 in *A True Relation of the Wonderful Cure of Mary Maillard*, accompanied by ten affidavits sworn by different persons before the Lord Mayor and by a long letter from J. Wellwood to the Lady Mayoress. A second tract of the same year and equally extensive entitled *Light in Darkness* is well described in its alternate title as 'a modest enquiry into, and humble improvement of Miracles, in general, upon occasion of this late miraculous cure of Mariane Maillard'. A fuller account, including a

---

[1] Loc. cit. p. 84. I suspect that like the next item which I mention, Howe's letter was not a private letter but a printed piece which I have not yet identified.

further testimony by the girl herself, now grown and married, was issued in 1730,[1] and there was a further edition in 1787.

Longer compilations of material of this sort were becoming characteristic in the late decades of the seventeenth century, and they usually relied on earlier published material. *The Miscellanies* of John Aubrey originally published in 1696 contained a section of 'Miranda' dealing with various cures. There are nine summary paragraphs ending with the account of Mary Maillard. The others were cures by a seventh son, by a dead hand, and by May-dew from a tombstone, and of course cures by the royal touch. Under this heading cures by the Duke of Monmouth are repeated, and the cure of Arise Evans by Charles II with the same personal attestation: 'Mr Ashmole told me'.

In the following year a mammoth collection, started thirty years before by Matthew Poole, author of a well-known Biblical collection called *Synopsis Criticorum*, was continued and completed by William Turner and published by John Dunton. It was called *A Compleat History of the Most Remarkable Providences both of Judgment and Mercy*, etc., and contained 150 chapters in four alphabets of over 600 folio pages.[2] Chapter LXXXII contains (pp. 108–20) thirty 'miraculous cures of diseases, etc.' of which several are familiar to us. Nos. 20–28 correspond to the items published by Aubrey. Nos. 15–19 are derived from Mather's sermon. No. 4 is the story of Marianne Maillard. No. 6 is that of Jeske Claes (taken from Glanvill). No. 2 is derived from Bishop Joseph Hall's *Mystery of Godliness*. No. 15 is from a French book published in 1687, while no. 30 reproduced in full a work published in 1696 (two editions) entitled *An Account of one Anne Jefferies now living in the*

---

[1] *An Exact Relation of the Wonderful Cure of Mary Maillard (now Wife of the Rev'd Mr. Henry Briel).*

[2] There are several references to misfortunes or follies of early Quakers in ch. LXXXVI of this volume, which is entitled: 'Satan Permitted to Hurt the Good in their Souls'. Cf. *J.F.H.S.* (1912), vol. IX, p. 83.

*County of Cornwall, who was fed for Six Months by a small
sort of Airy People, called Fairies: and of the strange and
wonderful Cures she performed with Salves and Medicines
she received from them for which she never took one Penny
of her Patients. In a Letter from Moses Pitt, to the Right
Reverend Father in God, Dr Edward Fowler, Lord Bishop of
Gloucester.* Several remaining pieces (nos. 3, 5, 11, 12, 13)
may be without printed antecedents. They are typical
stories of contemporary cures.

Curiously connected with this large work is an earlier
and smaller one, well known to students of colonial New
England. In 1684 Increase Mather published at Boston
*An Essay for the Recording of Illustrious Providences...
especially in New England.* He explains how some twenty-
six years before Matthew Poole and other ministers in
England or Ireland had planned such a work. But only a
MS. draft of it was then prepared. This MS. came to
America to John Davenport, and after his death Mather
found it and communicated it to other American ministers,
who contributed orally or in writing the incidents here
recorded. The sections on witchcraft are the best known
part, but only part of this book. Its ch. XI, 'Concerning
Remarkable Judgements', includes primarily judgements upon the Quakers—which did not go unanswered.
Only one episode recorded in it approximates the category of a miraculous cure, that of Abigail Eliot already
mentioned.[1]

Written more from the standpoint of medicine than
miracle, though of course impregnated with the attitude of
religious faith or resignation, was the large unpublished
work of Cotton Mather, entitled, like a smaller anonymous
published work of 1722, *The Angel of Bethesda.* Only one
section, that dealing with cures resulting from angelic

[1] Ch. II (at the beginning). Ch. I, 'Of Remarkable Sea Deliverances',
includes the episode of the fish and the great bird mentioned above. There
are references in this book to earlier works of the kind which I forbear to
name, still less to quote. On the history of this Essay of Mather, see Thomas
J. Holmes, *Increase Mather: a Bibliography of His Works* (1931), pp. 232–49.

instructions or inward impulses, belongs in the present category. Four of the five cures given are American rather than 'outlandish'.[1]

ATTACKS ON PUBLISHED MIRACLES

Some suggestion of what kind of controversy would have followed publication of Fox's 'Book of Miracles' may be seen from the Quakers' own controversial writings. Thus about 1672 a whole series of pamphlets were exchanged between various Friends and two Baptist pastors, Ralph James of Panton in Lincolnshire and Richard Hobbs of Dover in Kent.[2] The Baptist claims are adequately summarized by Thomas Rudyard:

> That one Richard Anderson, a Quaker, disputing with James whether the Spirit was to try Scripture, or the Scripture the Spirit; that R.A. avering the first, and he, the said R.J. being of the contrary opinion, that R.A. should say that he had the authority to pronounce him (that is R.J.) a Leper, and that within a short time after the Lord was pleased to smite one of R.A.'s children spotted all over, himself, his wife and his other children with a restless pain in their bodies; so that he was forced to come again and confess he was deceived and that R. Anderson should afterwards come to the Anabaptist publick meeting where the congregation prayed for him, his wife and children and that thereupon they were all restored to health, which afterwards R.A. keeping to their meetings confessed.[3]

This was obviously not merely a case of cure but of a miraculous judgement previously inflicted by smiting the Quaker and his family. As in other Baptist stories related above the cure was effected by the congregation at prayer.

---

[1] Pp. 74 ff., 'Capsule VIII. Raphael, or Notable Cures, from the Invisible World'. The manuscript is at the American Antiquarian Society, Worcester, Massachusetts. Cf. Thomas J. Holmes, *Cotton Mather: a Bibliography of his Works* (1940), vol. I, p. 44, for information about it.

[2] The literature is listed in Joseph Smith's *Bibliotheca Anti-Quakeriana* (1873), pp. 231–2, 250–1. The Quaker replies came from Luke Howard, Thomas Rudyard, Robert Ruckhill, William Smith and John Whitehead.

[3] *The Anabaptist's Lying Wonder* (1672), p. 3.

Introduction

The Quaker answer is mainly on matters of fact. The prior judgement resulting in leprosy and illness was denied rather than the cure and—most voluminously—it was asserted that Richard Anderson was not ever a Quaker. But in addition the Quaker writers urged that the story was intended to discredit them and to exalt the Baptists. They criticized producing this story to the light so many years afterwards—six and ten years are each suggested— and obviously felt that Ralph James told it to his own glory and produced in its support, in spite of certain testimonies, no real evidence, 'no eye and ear witnesses'. Indeed, James himself says that he had not made the matter public, thinking that it would be thought that he 'had gloried in it'.

The Friends evidently found the whole story inconsistent. Rudyard writes again:

> The first piece of abuse (I mean that out of Lincolnshire) presents the World with a miracle, and I must say a strange one too, a leprosie and diseased family miraculously cured by them whose known and owned belief and principle are that miracles are ceased: which exceeds the very power of Christ's Apostles, that could not so much as cure the lunatick having not faith, Mat. 17. 16, 17. And again that they should be so kind to a Quaker and his family as to cure them, whom of all persons they hate and which of all persons (they say) have not faith, is beyond all bounds of romance. And this ushered in as late piece of strange providence, and finger of heaven, of few days' or weeks' standing before publication, although the cheat was eight or nine, some say twelve, years past acted by those Water Baptists and now brought to light to their shame and their sophistry discovered by W.S. in answer to Ralph James his Subterfuge to which I refer the enquirer.[1]

[1] Thomas Rudyard, *The Water-Baptists Reproach Repel'd* (1673), pp. 41 f., in Luke Howard's *The Seat of the Scorner Thrown Down*. The books mentioned at the end are Ralph James, *The Quakers Subterfuge or Evasion Over-turned* (1672), and William Smith, *The Baptist's Sophistry Discovered* (1672/3). The other associated controversy which began with exchanges between Richard Hobbs and Luke Howard had to do with false prophecies more than with miracles on the part of Charles Bayly, a Friend who 'ran out'. Though even there Hobbs insisted against Howard that Bayly 'pretended to miracles' as well as prophesying and seeing false visions and that he was at that time or

The controversy had also its negative side. A year or two later the Baptists and the Quakers met for a noteworthy debate at the Barbican, and now the Quakers were challenged because they could show no miraculous signs wrought among them. George Whitehead, replying on behalf of the Quakers is satisfied with a *tu quoque* reply: 'At this rate how will you Baptists escape your own condemnation of being no Christians, or members of Christ's Church, if you cannot exhibit such an evidence as the gift of tongues inspired among you?'[1]

There is no better evidence of the kind of criticism to which Quakerism would have been exposed had the 'Book of Miracles' been published than is furnished by a survey of references to Fox's *Journal* with its miracles in some of the writings of Francis Bugg (1640–1724), 'the bitterest and most persistent of all the relapsed Quakers', who 'poured forth a stream of abusive books and pamphlets—over sixty in all—between 1680, when he became disaffected to Friends, and his death more than forty years later, an old man of eighty-four'.[2]

Although Fox's *Journal* was published in 1694, Bugg's watchful eye caught the miracle passages in it in time for printed comment long before the year was out. In reprinting his *New Rome Arraigned* both in his preface, dated 25 June 1694 and in his 'Apologitical' (*sic*) introduction, he mentions the miracles in this 'Alcoran' or 'Quakers Golden Calf or Legend of stories, viz. G. Fox's Journal'. Referring explicitly to the list of passages noted 'in the Third Table, under the word Miracles', he complains that

at least recently had been in good standing among Friends. See Luke Howard, *Love and Truth* (1703), p. 149. At p. 105 the date is given as October 1661, when Bayly and Howard were both prisoners at Dover.

[1] George Whitehead, *The Quakers' Plainness* (1674), pp. 13 f. Thomas Thompson, *The Quakers Quibbles* (1674). Second Part, Section III.

[2] W. C. Braithwaite, *The Second Period of Quakerism* (1919), p. 487. Bugg himself says he was a Quaker 25 years (*The Quakers Set in their True Light* (1696), p. 18), that in 1698 it was more than 20 years since he first wrote against them (*The Pilgrim's Progress from Quakerism to Christianity*, pp. 105, 157 f., referring to papers he sent in 1678 and in 1675).

not one of them is 'said to be done in the name of Jesus of Nazareth as in Acts 3. 6'; that the cure of the constable reported lacks all reference to the constable's name, his disease, or the town where he lived, and though pretended to be wrought in 1666 is exposed to public view in print in 1694, which shows it to be a fabulous story; and that their pretence to miracles equates the Quakers with the Papists. Bugg concludes: 'I have not room to shew the Tendency of those blasphemous Pretences of that Imposter G. Fox, which probably hereafter I may.'[1]

In 1696 Bugg returns again to the 'counterfeit miracles' in Fox's *Journal*. Of the 'many miracles' referred to on p. 167 Fox mentions neither where nor upon whom they took place; while of those more definitely recorded one, said to be wrought on a Parliament man in Maryland, is spoiled by the fact that there is no Parliament there, and to read the story of John Jay's broken neck, '*'twould make a melancholy man laugh'. It 'was all I, I, I and my, my, not a word of prayer'. In short they are all feigned, counterfeit miracles, and none done (as Erasmus well observes of Simon Magus) in the name of Jesus of Nazareth. Bugg also compares Fox's miracles with those claimed for Ignatius Loyola.[2]

[1] *New Rome Arraigned* (2nd ed. 1694), Preface, and pp. 2 f. Two earlier works by Friends are cited as mentioning miracles, viz. *A Reply to the Vindication &c.* p. 14: 'Visible Miracles have been done amongst us in the sight of the World' (pp. 2 and 66) and the epistle styled *This is Only to go Amongst Friends*. The latter was written by Francis Howgill in 1655 and refers I think only to miracles of conversion. The other piece was published in 1658 by Fox. In 1693, even before the *Journal* of Fox was published, Bugg in his first edition of this work had noted these two Quaker references to their working miracles, which had 'been found mere fictions to delude the people' (p. 2), and refers to a still earlier polemic of his own against them. The former of the two passages was cited by Bugg in *Some of the Quakers Principles and Doctrines, Laws and Orders*, 1693, p. 2. In 1691 he had spoken of the likelihood that the Quakers would match the Papists' feigned miracles (*Battering Rams against New Rome*, pp. 17, 23, 24).

[2] *The Quakers Set in their True Light* (1696), pp. 12 f., 18. As there was an assembly in Maryland in 1672, either Bugg is misinformed about it or he is quibbling over a name. In that case the blame is Ellwood's who has written in the passage (1694, p. 373), 'Parliament or Assembly' in place of the single word 'Assembly' of his source (as the three extant MSS. have it).

Introduction

In 1696 Croese's history of Quakerism had been published in English. Its reference to miracles of Fox, especially to that of John Jay, led Bugg back in 1697 to the subject. Again he urges that (*a*) though it is included in the index under the letter M 'Miracles wrought by the Power of God', actually it is described by Fox as 'wrought in his own Name, *I, I, I*, did so and so, and not as the Apostles did, "In the name of Jesus of Nazareth arise"'. (*b*) 'This is said to be done in 1672 and brought to light but in 1694 which is 22 years after it was said to be done.'[1] (*c*) 'This story of John Jay is surely as idle and unworthy of being esteemed a miracle as any thing can be found in the Popish legends; for if setting a man's neck aright, that had gone awry by a fall, be a miracle, then many miracles have been wrought in England and elsewhere, for it is very common, and yet was never called a miracle until now that these who published his Journal have so called it; and like to this is that one recovered from Sickness after G Fox had prayed, and if this was a Miracle, many such miracles are wrought by Ministers of the Church of England and others.'[2] (*d*) 'Many Friends though formerly they did not take much notice of them, now that they are called to their attention, believe that they may be a means of shaking the confidence of some well wishers to Quakerism, as well as doubting them themselves, as if done in a corner, nobody knows where nor when, otherwise than by his own relation. Never published till many years after they are said to be done. They were wrought in his own Name only, and not in the name of Jesus of Nazareth. Here is not one cripple that ever he cured, nor one dead Person that ever he raised, nor one blind that ever he gave sight to, to come forth and avouch that he was cured, was raised, was blind & now sees; and to be very plain, I do not believe there never was anything of a Miracle at all, but

---

[1] *A Brief History of the Rise, Growth, and Progress of Quakerism* (1697), p. 71. This is to be distinguished from the last-named work, though that has a very similar sub-title and running head.

[2] Ibid. p. 73 ff.

only an Artifice to hold the people in admiration of G Fox, etc.'[1]

Slight references to the miracles of the Quakers appear in a publication of 1698. Fox 'writ them in his own name, like those of Simon Magus, and certain vagabond Jews, exorcists; but these lying wonders came too late, some 20, some 30 years after they were said to be done nobody knows, where, nor when, nor who were cured, nor no witness to attest the truth thereof.'[2]

In the work just quoted Francis Bugg refers (p. 160) to a 'Book, intituled, *News of a Trumpet sounding in the Wilderness, &c.* which is come lately out of Pensilvania, Printed 1697', and expresses the hope that it would be 'reprinted, with this Title, *A Trumpet sounding from Pensilvania giving an Alarum to the Magistrates & People of England to beware of Quakerism*'. This work, a Bradford imprint now very rare, was by Daniel Leeds, 'who had been a Quaker about 20 years', but had joined the party of George Keith. Since it appeared in 1699 in London, not in reprint but simply with a new title-page giving London booksellers and a new title almost identical with that proposed by Bugg, we may include it in this chronological review upon the assumption that Bugg instigated the London edition. Indeed, his own earlier books had evidently suggested much of Leeds' material. Chapter XIII deals with Quaker miracles. According to Leeds they are either blasphemous, or else are ordinary events. For example, Leeds knew John Jay personally and spoke with him afterwards, but regarded the re-setting of his neck, 'such a thing as that many have done, yea, a prophane man has done the like to my knowledge'. When he had recently

---

[1] *A brief History of the Rise, Growth, and Progress of Quakerism.* (1697), pp. 160 ff. In the Quaker replies to Bugg one of the few discussions of his repeated 'charge of blasphemous pretenses of miracles against G.F.' was published in 1697, presumably by George Whitehead. See *A Sober Expostulation with some of the Clergy*, pp. 48 f.

[2] *The Pilgrim's Progress from Quakerism to Christianity* (1698), pp. 25, 29 (with list of pages in the *Journal*); 2nd ed. 1700, pp. 53, 61 (where 'writ' is corrected to 'wrought' by the errata at the end of the preface).

heard of real miracles wrought in London he was afraid
that they would be claimed by the Quakers, already too
insolent, and was relieved to hear that one was wrought on
a French Protestant girl that was lame (evidently Mary
Maillard), the other on a Baptist woman who had leprosy
(perhaps the widow Susanna Arch whom Mather tells of).
Leeds accepts the possibility of miracles worked upon the
truly pious. Indeed, he prints a letter of endorsement
which mentions Leeds himself as having recovered
miraculously from an extreme impediment of stammering.[1]

In 1700 Bugg again refers to 'Fox's miracles in his
Journal published thirty or forty years after they are said
to be wrought and no body can tell me where, nor when,
nor the persons names cured, or any witness to attest
them...never an one of which are said to be wrought in
the name of Jesus, but only in his own name and by his
own power, like Simon Magus'.[2]

In an anonymous work of the same year, written, I
think, by Bugg, the author makes much the same criticism
of Fox's claim to miracles, again using the story of John
Jay as an illustration; but he compares them not with the
deeds of Simon Magus but with the miraculous legends of
the Papists.[3]

In 1701 Bugg writes a humorous and sarcastic dialogue
among three Quakers, of whom one, George Whitehead—
who was Bugg's special aversion—is made to list, among
thirty-two things which he said the Inner Light had
taught Friends to believe, that 'Fox wrought many

---

[1] *News of a Trumpet*, pp. 108–13, 143. *Satan's Harbinger*, by Caleb
Pusey (1700), in replying to this book does not deal with the miracles at
length. But in answer to the charge against Fox of blasphemy or pride he
asserts (p. 81): 'I am satisfied that where at any time G.F. in his Journal hath
mentioned any Miracle which God wrought by him, the intent was not to
set up or applaud the Creature nor to boast of the work but to give the
praise and honor to God the worker, to whom it belongs.'

[2] *A Modest Defence of my Book, entituled Quakerism Expos'd* (1700), pt. III,
p. 8.

[3] *A Parallel between the Faith and Doctrine of the Present Quakers and
that of the chief Hereticks in all Ages of the Church, and also a Parallel
between Quakerism and Popery* (1700), pp. 45 f.

miracles, as in his Journal', but urges that Friends should 'make no noise of these things, nor of his Glister-Pipe he bequeathed to Doctor Lower, the great Quaker doctor'.[1]

In 1702 Fox's miracles are again mentioned, and the reader referred as usual to the index to the *Journal* with its list of cures and pages. But Francis Bugg has now another episode to add. It is not in Fox's *Journal*, but it is a story known to us from other sources which have already been discussed above.[2] Bugg's characteristic version of it may be worth quoting:

> I shall give one single instance, to mention no more. About twenty or two and twenty years since there was a Quaker of Amsterdam named Cornelius Rolloffs, who hearing of a madman in North Holland or Friezland, believed he had power given him to cure him; upon which he takes a journey to him, and as Elisha spread himself upon the dead child, so did he, and put his nose to his nose, his mouth to his mouth, and stretching himself; and no doubt called hard upon his Light within. However, though he could not cure the madman, for he remained mad still, yet he received the poison of the madman's madness, and thereby grew mad and was put into the madman's hospital and there continued mad to his dying day; and the madman still continued mad also. But this spoils the Quakers' miracles in those parts....There is many Quakers in Holland remembers this passage very well; but if they deny it, I have it well attested by credible evidence now living in London.[3]

In 1707, taking again the twelve miracles listed in the index to Fox's *Journal*, Bugg discusses each in turn and makes the same kind of criticism as before—lack of detail, lapse of time, lack of witnesses, inconsistency or contradiction.[4]

As late as 1720 I find Bugg quoting the Quakers' claim to have the power that Christ had: 'By it miracles are wrought. For now do the blind see, the deaf hear...and

---

[1] *News from New Rome* (1701), pp. 48 f.   [2] Pp. 30 f.

[3] *A Narrative of the Conference at Sleeford in Lincolnshire* (1702), pp. 150 f.

[4] *Hidden Things Brought to Light* (1707), § vii, being pt. iii in *A Finishing Stroke* (1712), pp. 192–8.

this we witness to be fulfilled within us.'[1] Probably here as in some other places the Quakers should be understood as referring to figurative or spiritual cures. But it is significant that Bugg cites not the *Journal* of Fox, but much earlier pamphlets. Obviously he did not know a book that would have been so much more to his purpose if he had known it—the manuscript 'Book of Miracles'. For at least thirty years after Fox's death it was not accessible to his critics.

Although the printed edition of Fox's *Journal* represents already in 1694 some editorial caution in the matter of miracles—omissions from the manuscript and verbal changes such as we have already mentioned—its later circulation and reprinting indicate no anxiety on the part of Friends with respect to the criticisms that Francis Bugg and others levelled against it. Nor did any conscientious Friends so far as we know raise doubt as to the veracity of its narratives of miraculous cure. This is all the more striking since we do know that two other statements in it were challenged and unusual pains taken to correct them. Both of them belong to the category of 'examples', similar but opposite to miracles.

Thus on p. 309 of the *Journal* is given an account of a Justice in Derbyshire who was particularly severe upon

---

[1] *A New Frame for the Picture of Quakerism* (1720), pt. IV, p. 144, with reference to [Fox and Nayler's] *A Word from the Lord* (1654) and [Hubberthorne's] *A True Separation* [1659?]. Some insight into Bugg's manner of using the writings of Friends may be obtained from a collection of over four hundred Quaker books and tracts bound in over forty volumes still extant in the Library of Christ Church, Oxford. Bugg's later writings tell how they were acquired from him for the college by Dean Aldrich. Some of them are extensively interlined or marked in the margin, while on the fly leaves Bugg has entered references to matters he could quote against Friends. Among passages so marked I have noted in the present connection the claim that Friends have the same power as was in Christ, 'for now do the blind see, the deaf hear, and the lame walk...the lepers are cured and the leprosy is taken away' (in the pamphlet just mentioned, *A True Separation*, p. 7), or 'The Lord hath opened our eyes without thy prayers' (George Fox and Hubberthorne, *Truth's Defense*, 1653, p. 45), or conversely the statement that Christ's miracles were but a shadow of inward miracles to come (Isaac Penington, *Concerning the Sum or Substance of our Religion* [c. 1667], p. 13).

Friends, especially upon Ellen Fretwell. The account concludes—with a characteristic index (☞) in the margin —as follows:

Susan Frith was moved to tell him, That if he continued on in this persecuting of the innocent the Lord would execute his plagues upon him. Soon after which, this Justice, whose name was Clark, fell distracted and was bound with ropes; but he gnawed the ropes in pieces and had like to have spoiled his maid: for he fell upon her and bit her; so that they were fain to put an iron instrument in his mouth to wrest his teeth out of her flesh: and afterwards he died distracted. This relation I had from Ellen Fretwell herself.[1]

But the Morning Meeting in London which was responsible finally for Quaker publication soon received a letter 'from several Friends in Derbyshire, signifying that they think the relation in G. Fox's Journal folio 309 should be left out, for they suspect the verity of part of the relation, and request it may be left out'. Accordingly it was decided to reprint the leaf (folios 309, 310) and to send copies of the new leaves 'to every county to a couple of discreet faithful Friends to take out the old leaves and put in the new as carefully and neatly as they can'.[2] The new leaf (and later printed editions) read, for the long middle sentence above, simply:

Soon after which he fell distracted and died in that state.

The other instance is less well known; it has in fact apparently never been published. It is recorded thus in the minutes of the same Second Day Morning Meeting:

The leaf 441, 442 in G.F.'s Journal is reprinted by the Friends of Holland, and they have sent over a parcel, which this meeting

---

[1] The wording in Ellwood is practically that of the manuscript (printed in II, 109); the details are also given in the MS. volumes of 'Sufferings' at Friends' House, I, 329.

[2] MS. Minutes of the Morning Meeting. Extracts in Joseph Smith, *Descriptive Catalogue of Friends' Books*, vol. I, p. 691; *Friends' Quarterly Examiner* (1902), p. 67; Cambridge *Journal*, vol. II, p. 405. Many extant copies contain the new leaf and show how neatly it was prepared and inserted. But to judge from more than fifty copies of this edition which I have examined in England and America, the great majority never received the new leaf.

Introduction

having viewed do approve of and desire Thomas Lower, Mark Swanner and Thomas Northcott to consider in whose hands any books may be to use any of the said papers. William Warren hath 7 for York city and country.[1]

In the leaf named, reference is made to the city of Frederick-stadt as follows:

> This city is in the Duke of Holstein's country, who would have banished Friends out of the city and country, and did send to the magistrates of the city to do it.... And not long after, the Duke himself was banished out of that city, by the King of Denmark.

Here again was an example of retributive judgement upon a persecutor of Quakers and again local Friends took exception to it, whether as unwise or untrue. If an error of fact, it would do the Quaker cause great harm. The substitute leaf simply left out the last-quoted sentence.[2]

In contrast to these instances the miracle narratives in Fox's *Journal* remain unchanged. When in 1709 a second edition was called for all the things that the enemies of Quakerism had criticized in the first edition are reprinted verbatim.

The claim to work miracles often recoils like a boomerang upon the claimant. There was always the possibility that the same marvel was due to an evil rather than to a good spirit. Theologians strove in vain to distinguish between miracles wrought by the Divine power only and the kind of miracles which Satan worked. Witchcraft[3] and magic were not denied in the seventeenth century, and Fox and other Friends were repeatedly suspected of the black arts.

---

[1] MS. Minutes of the Morning Meeting, 27th of 11 mo. 1695 [January, 1696].

[2] None of the exemplars of Fox's *Journal* mentioned in the earlier note has the substitute page and I have yet to see a copy of it. The change can be inferred from the changed reading in later editions of the *Journal*. The original edition followed the manuscript source accurately enough (III, 244—the *Haistwell Diary* of Fox's journey to the Continent in 1677), but a letter of Willem Sewel in 1694 implies that the Duke had rather promptly repented of his earlier harsh treatment of the Quakers (W. I. Hull, *Willem Sewel of Amsterdam*, p. 128).

[3] Cf. G. L. Kittredge, *Witchcraft in Old and New England*, p. 587.

Even if the truth of Quakers' miracles was not denied, it was possible to attribute them to the working of Satan and so equally well discredit them.[1]

The fastings of Friends were reported by their enemies as well as by their admirers. The capacity to live without food was certainly uncanny and perhaps worse. The Quarter Sessions records when they quote complaints against Friends as vagabonds often add that they appear to live without visible means of support—a fact which might sometimes imply the secret support of their human conspirators, but sometimes the diabolical capacity to be kept alive without food.[2] Other testimony had the same tendency—to discredit the Quakers, while tacitly admitting their magical or miraculous practices. I cite the information of John Forshoe of Over Whitley taken 13 February 1655/6 telling how a Quaker neighbour, William Mosse, a tailor, tried to warn him against the established worship.

Telling him that if he had been carried on a black horse as Mosse had, he would not follow Mr Elcocke the minister nor that steeple house, meaning Budworth Church. And that if this informant were longer by Mr Elcocke he would be led by the Divell, but wished this informant to follow their ways, meaning the Quakers, and he should be led by the Spiritt, which this informant utterly refused, and said he was in a good way already. But Mosse further told this informant that he had been mounted on a black horse and carried from the further side of Barterton Heath to Adam Eaton's House in Appleton and from there to Heywood's and thence to John

---

[1] The reality of the cures might go unquestioned, as is shown by a case in the session records of Aberdeen in 1681 where one woman confessed that she had cured another by using as a charm a hose and tying a thread about it and putting the hose about the patient (*Records of Old Aberdeen* (1909), vol. II, pp. 74 f.). Fox was called a witch as early as 1652 (I, 104). He was charged soon after with hanging ribbons on people's arms and making them follow him (I, 169). Cf. A. N. Brayshaw, *The Personality of George Fox* (1933), pp. 68–70. This report was put in print and was echoed as late and as far away as Barbados and New England in 1672.

[2] So Thomas Salthouse, arrested at Compton Pauncefoot 24 April 1657 had been wandering up and down the Western Counties being sent by the Eternal God and had both food and raiment though without visible means of subsistence. E. H. B. Harbin, *Quarter Sessions Records for the County of Somerset* (Somerset Record Society (1912), vol. XXVIII, p. 339).

Eaton's neere Weverham and afterwards the horse threw him over three great thorne hedges, as most were, and there was left, and since that time Moss told him he was enlightened.[1]

Amelia M. Gummere has collected various examples of the contemporary literary attacks upon Quakerism as given to witchcraft and magic.[2] The charges against Fox included his use of enchanted bracelets and pillows, while others were accused of more destructive forms of magic. That Fox believed he could discern in others an evil spirit or even witchcraft is sufficiently attested. It was natural that his opponents speaking from the background of the same period should have from the first turned the charge against him and his followers. The claim to work miracles by the finger of God has long been exposed to the counter explanation of casting out demons by Beelzebub.

Had Friends in London published after 1694 the 'Book of Miracles', there would have been similar insinuations made. Why had they kept it so long unpublished? In spite of some signed certificates of witnesses, its stories at this late date could not be authenticated. Some went back over forty years, most of them at least twenty years and several were said to have taken place in distant America. Furthermore, the whole manner of the book was to glorify Fox as the miracle-worker. This criticism we know was made against the miracles in the *Journal* in spite of corrective revisions in the text made by Thomas Ellwood and the pious wording of the index, s.v. 'Miracles'.

The want of printed records of Quaker miracles is noted by Jonathan Clapham, one of the opponents, as early as 1656. Contrasting the Quakers with the Papists who published their miracles and with some Anabaptists at Whatfield in Suffolk who 'published a book called the Gospel Way Confirmed by Miracles, the notorious falsehood of which was afterwards confessed before B. Gurdon, Esq.,

---

[1] *Quarter Sessions Records...for the County Palatine of Chester 1559–1760* (Record Society of Lancashire and Cheshire (1940), vol. xciv, p. 164).

[2] *Witchcraft and Quakerism, A Study in Social History* (1908), pp. 30 f. The book is full of interesting collateral data.

Justice of the Peace there, and their confessions published Anno 1649', he explains their silence thus:

> It's true that they have not yet published any volumes of their miracles to the world in print....They pretend to learn modesty from the example of Christ, who forbad the reporting of many of his miracles to the world; but they make no little use of them among their seduced ones to confirm them thereby in their delusions, and its not unlikely would make them more publick to the world were it not that they feared to be found liars if they should do so.[1]

Gerard Croese is not usually a reliable reporter of Quakerism, and especially not in more delicate matters like this. But his words, even if largely his own expansion of cautions suggested in the Quaker sources available, may fairly represent the Quaker attitude when he wrote, at a time which is almost exactly contemporary with the date from which our evidence of the 'Book of Miracles' comes. After citing two miracles related by Fox himself, and another which he says 'his Friends added', he mentions the Quaker claim to visions and prophecies and continues:

> The Quakers who succeeded these first beginners do not make so much noise either of Miracles or Visions, nor do they willingly speak or write of those of their Sect that preceded them, unless very cautiously and warily; acknowledging and owning that since the old Gospel preached by Christ and his Apostles was sufficiently confirmed with Miracles and Predictions, this new Gospel, which they now advance, being in substance the same with that of old, does not need these Helps and Miracles: That they do not make their Religion depend upon them; that they neither hope nor wish for Praise and Glory from Men, nor expect to procure a favourable Reception from them upon any such account. So that it seems this is their intention to boast of some of the Signs of the Primitive

---

[1] Jonathan Clapham, *A Full Discovery*, etc. (1656), p. 44. The book of Baptist miracles which he cites is not known to modern Baptist bibliographers, but something of its contents may be inferred from the recantation *A Brief Representation and Discovery of An notorious falshood and dissimulation contained in a Book styled, The Gospel-Way confirmed by Miracles*, published by Nicholas Ware and Matthew Hall (London, 1649) of which a copy is in the British Museum. The woman whom these preachers claimed to have cured admitted that it was all a hoax, 'but jugglings and collusions'.

and Apostolick Church, but withal to take care lest if these Signs be not clear and manifest to all, they should come to be despised and laughed at: Unless they propose to themselves the Example of our Saviour who sometimes took pains to conceal his Miracles and Prophecies.[1]

Whatever the reason may have been—and we must remember that the original plans for publishing all of Fox's writings were abandoned when only three folio volumes had been published (*Journal*, 1694; *Epistles*, 1698; *Doctrinals*, 1706)—evidently the 'Book of Miracles' was never printed. The first references to it are in the *Journal* MS. but later than 1675 when that was mostly written. The last references are those in the *Annual Catalogue*, key and index. These apparently are written in 1694 to 1698. No later reference to the book is known. Whether by intention or by accident it has been, as far as we know, long lost. Norman Penney, to whom the data in the *Annual Catalogue* were not known, called attention to one possible though uncertain reference to the book in 1735. He wrote:[2]

We have searched in vain for any 'book of miracles' among extant Quaker records, but we have recently found what may be a reference to such a book in *A Short Account of the People called Quakers*, by Henry Pickworth. Pickworth, ex-Quaker, was detailing what he believed to be parallel views held by Friends ('Foxonian Quakers') and the Family of Love or Familists, under the leadership of Henry Nicholas, and among many 'authorities' for this similarity of doctrine and practice, he gives: '*Private Miracles in Manuscript*' (p. 50). This may refer to a copy of 'The Book of Miracles', and is the only reference we have found to such a collection after the references in *The Journal* MSS. What a find it would be if the Book should re-appear!

As a partial fulfilment of his hope this study is published and dedicated to his memory.

---

[1] *General History of the Quakers* (Engl. tr. 1696), pp. 28 f.

[2] *J.F.H.S.* (1925), vol. XXII, p. 94. In the same work (p. 16) Pickworth refers to Fox's 'pretences to miracles', but the context suggests that he has in mind those in the printed *Journal* of Fox's life.

ADDENDA TO FOOTNOTES

Page 21, *note* 4. Perhaps the next earliest reference in print to a miracle by Fox is to his curing a woman of the King's Evil, in *Twenty Quaking Queries*, 1659, p. 4.

Page 22, *note* 2. A Quaker account of a painless delivery is reported by letter from Thomas Salthouse to Margaret Fell (Swarthmore MSS. iii, 158; Olveston, Glos., 9 September 1657): 'This day I came [from Worcester] about 30 miles to Walter Clements' house who is at liberty and well. And this very hour, being about the seventh hour at night is Walter Clements' wife delivered of a daughter by the mighty power of the Lord. Before she travailed she brought forth [Isaiah lxvi. 7] to the astonishment of the heathen that cannot believe and to the praise and honor of him that hath taken away the curse [Genesis iii. 16] and redeemed his own from under the transgression, who is present with healing in his wings' [Malachi iv. 2], etc.

Page 26, *note* 5. The demand for miracles and the Quaker reply is already presented in 1655 by John Whitehead, writing from Northampton gaol in his autobiographical essay *The Enmity between the Two Seeds* (p. 9, reprinted in *The Written Gospel Labours of...John Whitehead*, 1904, p. 13; cf. Thomas Chalk, *Life and Writings of John Whitehead*, 1852, p. 26). The non-Quakers say: 'If you be sent as the Apostles were, and have the same spirit that they had, show us a Sign or a Miracle, that we may see it and believe: But I say unto you that seek after a Sign that all that had the same Spirit, and by it did witness the Truth, did not work Miracles.'

Page 29, *note* 1. Robert Barclay's earliest printed work, *Truth Cleared of Calumnies*, 1670, p. 57 (*Works*, 1692, pp. 36-7; 1718, I, 68-9; 1831, I, 199-200) deals at length with this subject, as does William Mitchell in works preceding and following this reply of Barclay's.

Page 45. On Sewel's restraint in citing miracles see W. I. Hull, *Willem Sewel of Amsterdam*, 1933, p. 184, where Robert Southey's commendation is quoted. Yet writing to Gerard Croese in 1692 Sewel offered to tell him of the miraculous experience of some girls who had been ill (*ibid.*, pp. 120f.).

Page 70, *note* 1. It was natural that Friends should include in their ministrations those who were in mental discomfort and that without any claim of the miraculous they should expect that by calling attention to the Christian message they could assuage despair and relieve mental distress. Such service they believed settled or stayed the mind at least for a time. For example, John Whitehead adds a postscript in a letter to William Dewsbury: 'There is a young woman at Sherrington in much distress and distraction of spirit nigh to be overwhelmed with desperation. I was there yesternight and the witness was touched in measure to stay her mind. If thou hast opportunity it may be in service to her.' (Dewsbury Correspondence, No. 19; Newport [Pagnell], 28 January 1656.)

Page 78, *note* 2. A pamphlet of 1649, entitled *A Miracle of Miracles*, served a like political purpose by relating a cure of blindness, due to the King's Evil, by use of a handkerchief dipped in the blood of Charles I.

Page 89, *note* 2. In *The Principles of the Quakers, Further shown to be Blasphemous and Seditious*, 1700, pp. 41-3, Edward Beckham and two other rectors in Norfolk deal with the Quaker attitude to miracles, and suggest that in contrast with earlier pretenses to miracles Friends 'now begin to be ashamed of their pretenses to them, and to lessen their authority as much as may be'. George Whitehead's reply is in his *Truth Prevalent*, 1701, pp. 81-3.

THE 'BOOK OF MIRACLES'

The main entries below are printed as nearly as possible as they are given in one or more places in the index to the *Annual Catalogue* of George Fox. An asterisk (*) is added after each of the words under which the passages are cited in the index, often two or three different words for each item. The number given to each item is the page of the original MS. 'Book of Miracles' to which the index assigned its entry. When the same item is assigned to two successive pages, I have assumed that it ran over from the first to the second and have numbered it so. To distinguish the several items on the same page letters of the alphabet have been added to the page number. The order of the items so arranged on a page is usually arbitrary. Only in a few cases does the index indicate the original order of these items.

Where the actual text of the rest of the item has been identified it has been printed in square brackets between the index entries. Where parallel accounts are found in Fox's *Journals*, one for each item is printed in smaller type after the entry from the 'Book of Miracles'. Some other parallels are included in the notes.

For persons who are discussed in Norman Penney's biographical notes to the *Journals* or elsewhere, references to these latter are merely given in the notes. For other persons the largest available lists of Friends have been Joseph Besse, *A Collection of the Sufferings of the People of God called Quakers from 1650 to 1689* (2 vols. London, 1753), and the printed list of more than 7000 women who signed protests against tithes whose title begins: *These Several Papers was Sent to the Parliament the 20th Day of the 5th Moneth, 1659.*

The *Journals* of Fox are cited as follows: the Cambridge *Journal*, simply as I and II, representing the two volumes published by the Cambridge University Press in 1911. The *Short Journal and the Itinerary Journals* published by the same in 1925 is referred to simply as III. Of the editions of the *Journal* as first edited by Thomas Ellwood, the first edition (1694) and the bicentenary edition (1891 and later reprints) alone are used and are referred to by these years.

For other abbreviations see I, 391 ff. or III, xxxi ff.

7–8   Upon a time G.F. was at Evesham*...sickness*...
in the Lord's service.

8   When G.F. came into the country...Captain Bates*
of Carolina...physicians*...had done great things.

And many people of the world did receive us gladly and they
came to us at one Nathaniel Batts', formerly governor of Roanoke,
who goeth by the name of Captain Batts; who hath been a rude
desperate man.

He came to us and said that a captain told him that in Cumberland G.F. bid one of his friends go to a woman that had been sick
a long time, and all the physicians had left her, and could not heal
her. And G.F. bid his friend to lay his hands upon her and pray by
her, and that G.F.'s friend did go to the woman, and did as he bade
him, and the woman was healed that time.

And thus Captain Batts told me, and had spread it up and down
in the country among the people. And he asked me of it, and I
said many things had been done by the power of Christ.

II, 234 (North Carolina, 9th mo. 1672)

7–8   The Cambridge *Journal* mentions visits of Fox to Evesham in
1655, 1656 and 1660. He was probably there later also. It was from
Evesham in 1678 that Fox went to visit Lady Conway at Ragley (III, 267),
but there is no evidence that he relieved her illness.

8   This discussion with Batts is included in the Bristol MS., but in the
Bodleian MS. (*J.F.H.S.* (1912), vol. IX, p. 24) it is quite obscured in the
following form: 'He spread abroad relations that he said he heard from an
acquaintance of his of some passages of G.F. in England which affected the
people.' For Ellwood's revision of the passage, see above p. 42.

On Nathaniel Batts, see II, 442. The spelling Bates in the only entry for
the name in the index to the 'Book of Miracles' is found also in the printed
index to Fox's *Journal* (Ellwood, 1694). The Bodleian MS. adds a statement
of the Captain's 'great command' over that country especially over the
Indians which fits in with the other allusion to him by Fox in which,
writing in 1673 to Friends in Virginia he suggests: 'If you go over again to
Carolina you may inquire of Capt. Batts, the Old Governor, with whom I
left a Paper to be read to the Emperor and his Thirty Kings under him of the
Tuscaroras who were to come to treat for peace with the people of Carolina,
whether he did read it to them or no.' (*Epistles* (1698), p. 336—addressed
originally to William Denson according to MS. sources.) Can anyone else be
intended by 'the Governor of Carolina' in the list of persons designated by

8–9   G.F. being a prisoner at W[orcester]...Wood-cock*...infirmity*...worthy for ever. Amen.

9   The scales* of death was upon [my eyes that I could hardly see...who is worthy of all praise and glory for ever and for evermore.
G.F. his sickness and weakness in] Worcester prison.

George Fox in the same year to receive from him copies of the works of Edward Burrough (Bowden, *History of Friends in America*, vol. I, p. 358)?

Earlier Quaker editors and historians—Weeks, Penney, Hull and Jones—have been unable to tell us more of Governor Batts. There is, however, independent evidence to establish Nathaniel Batts as a resident of Albemarle who died intestate before 5 November 1679 when his widow now married to Joseph Chew was serving as executrix (*North Carolina Historical and Genealogical Register* (1900), vol. I, pp. 30, 612). In the archives at Edenton to which the latter citation refers he is associated with Hugh Smithwick, who in Fox's *Journal* appears as a near neighbour (half a mile away or a mile and a half. At II, 237 his name is spelled Smith and that has led Ellwood and other editors astray).

More recently in an article 'The Earliest Permanent Settlement in Carolina: Nathaniel Batts and the Comberford Map', *Amer. Hist. Rev.* (1939), vol. XLV, pp. 82 ff. Professor W. P. Cumming has collected evidence to show that Nathaniel Batts owned land in Nansemond County, Virginia, and had as early as 1657 been interested in exploration to the southward, and had already a house at the head of Roanoke Sound. There was a considerable settlement here also from Nansemond County before the charter of 1663 established a regular government, and in that settlement Batts was the leading man. In other places along the coast the nomenclature shows his influence.

8–9   On Jane Woodcock of London, see II, 453. With others she went in August 1674 to ask the King in person for the enlargement of George Fox, prisoner at Worcester (II, 299). Like this item, the three that follow are dated during his Worcester imprisonment.

9   The wording inside the brackets has been added from 91 N, a MS. now lost except as preserved in the index to the *Annual Catalogue*. For the illness of Fox in Worcester Prison when he was so weak as to be almost speechless and seemed to be among the corpses, see Ellwood, *Journal* (1694), p. 404; (1891), II, 227. An account more similar to this than to that was in the *Great Journal*, p. 748. See *Annual Catalogue*, p. 17, 92 F and 17, 93 F. The vision is there dated exactly upon 12th of 5 mo. 1674. The Headley MSS. had once, as their index shows, on initial pages now no longer extant under date of 1673, 'G.F. A Vision of his in Worcester prison' and 'G.F. A sight of his concerning the work of the Lord.'

The last line is a kind of endorsement. As in no. 10 *a* this is quoted in the text at the end of the episode. Cf. no. 33 *a*.

giles kendall m ... ther was broken
in his bely 4 yeres ... in great sorrow & mig
cry & as he was diging in his garding
in great raine he cryed vnto the lord
& sayd if hee would but speake the
word he beleued he should be well
& the lord answered him ... darkly he
was well & came a foot aboue 20
miles to wosfer to vifed ... in yreseni
an old man ner feventy & further
the faid giles ... all faid that their
was ... none ficke & the faid that
he would dy & giles faid he beleued
that he would not dy & he was moued
to pray for him & did beleue & had
faith in god that the lord would heal
him & the lord did & the ficke did
recouer & did not dy & he alfo
fpeake of a nother that was fick
which he had feath for & did ...
ouer the giles fpeake to mee in
wosfer yrefent mo: 10: day 30: 1674

VII. Account of Giles Kendall in Handwriting
of George Fox (No. 10a)

the testimonie of Gyles
Kendall of Glastoushon
concerning the word of the
Lord and his blessing
being healed by his beleife
therein

Endorsement in
Another Hand

10 *a*   Giles Kendall* in Gloucestershire [was broken in his belly four years and in great sorrow and misery. And as he was digging in his garden in great pain he cried unto the Lord and said if he would but speak the word he believed he should be well. And the Lord answered him and immediately he was well and came afoot above twenty miles to Worcester to visit G.F. in prison, an old man near seventy.

And farther the said Giles Kendall said that there was one sick and they said that he would die and Giles said he believed that he would not die, and he was moved to pray for him and did believe and had faith in God that the Lord would hear him and the Lord did and the sick did recover and did not die.

And he also spake of another that was sick* which he had faith for and did recover. This Giles spake to me in Worcester prison] mo. 10, day 30, 1674.

[The testimony of Giles Kendal of Gloucestershire concerning the word of the Lord and his being healed] by his belief therein.

10 *b*   There was a young maid of Colonel Ashford*... sick*...of God and his love. 1674.

---

10 *a*   This account in Fox's own handwriting is preserved in Friends' House, London, in Portfolio 36.169 (see plate opposite p. 102). The endorsement is in another hand, but that too was included in the 'Book of Miracles', since of the two entries in the index one quotes its last words, the other quotes the last words of the main narrative.

Besse, *Sufferings*, vol. I, p. 211, relates how Giles Kendall and others in January 1660/1 were arrested for attending meeting and were sent to the city gaol by the mayor and aldermen of Gloucester for refusing the oaths.

The registers of Gloucester Monthly Meeting record the death of Gellis Kendall, of Porton, on 23rd of 3 mo. 1683 and the burial at Cheltenham on 4th of 8 mo. 1691 of Ann Kendall of Porton, wife of Gilles. Among Gloucestershire wills probated in 1686 was that of Giles Kendall of Churchdown. See *A Calendar of Wills Proved in the Consistory Court of the Bishop of Gloucester*, II, 1660–1800 (*Index Library* (1907), vol. XXXIV, p. 53).

10 *b*   Colonel Ashford is not identified. Possibly Colonel Richard Ashfield is intended, a justice of the peace in Scotland in 1657 and governor of Glasgow. He became a Friend, a speaker among Friends and a meeting was held in his house. See I, 303, 453.

Fox's 'Book of Miracles'

11 *a*   G.F. was at a great meeting. . .Judge* (recovered)
. . .sick*. . .not long after very well.

And on the 27th day we passed by water 20 miles to a meeting
very large, some hundreds of the world and an establishing meeting
it was. . . . And after the meeting was done one a judge's wife that

---

11 *a*   The other manuscript accounts (Bodleian MS. and Bristol MSS.
v, 37 ff.) agree almost exactly in wording with what is printed above from
the MS. 'Epistles and Queries'. Ellwood in paraphrasing the account
writes: 'and I being just come hot out of the meeting, it was hard for me
then to go; yet considering the service I got an horse and visited her husband
and spake what the Lord gave me to him, and the man was much refreshed,
and finely raised up by the power of the Lord; and he afterwards came to
our meetings (1694, p. 373; 1891, ii, 179).

The identification of this judge and member of the Maryland Assembly
has apparently not been undertaken but it may be not altogether impossible.
The geographical data are not very clear. His home is described as three
miles 'down' from the place where a 'great meeting' had been held that
day. Unfortunately the name of that place is not given in any of the
manuscripts of this narrative, though one of them leaves a space for it
(*J.F.H.S.* (1912), vol. ix, p. 18). We shall call this place '*x*'. The context
shows by its accounts of Fox's movements before and after that he had
reached '*x*' by travelling twenty miles by water from Henry Wilcock's house
on the Kentish shore. But neither Henry Wilcock nor his house are otherwise
known to us. Fox had reached it by travelling twenty-two miles to John
Edmondson at Tred Avon (or Thirdhaven). His farm, Cedar Point, near the
present town of Easton, can apparently be located exactly but not so the home
of Fox's previous host, one Robert Harwood, described as on Miles River and
three or four miles away. For Harwood's earlier homes or holdings, see
Emerson B. Roberts, *Maryland Historical Magazine* (1942), vol. xxxvii,
p. 319. He was on the Eastern Shore by 1662, owned Cold Spring in
Dorchester County in 1664 and died in 1675. Returning now to '*x*', we find
that after the visit to the sick man Fox returned to the house there (private
house? or meeting house?) and by travelling from '*x*' 'about 5 miles by
water and then 14 miles by land' he came again to John Edmondson's.
These movements represent no travel in a consecutive line, but the varied
and often roundabout or criss-cross journeys in the broken land and water
areas of the eastern shore of Maryland.

In spite of this uncertainty it seems probable that all these places,
including both '*x*' and the home of the judge three miles away, were in
Talbot County, whose limits in 1672 are not exactly known but were
certainly much more extended than after Queen Anne County was set off in
1706 and Caroline County in 1773. What citizens of that county meet the
definition of Fox's patient?

Now Fox mentions notables galore in his Maryland narrative. There had
been a judge's wife at her first Friends' meeting near Robert Harwood's on
Miles River (22nd of 7 mo.) and one of the burgesses—one of three MSS.

side of the country, he is one of the assembly, she being at the
meeting desired to speak with me and desired me to go down with
her to her house, for her husband was sick and not like to live and
it was 3 miles. And it being after the meeting I was hot, but got

---

reads judges—at the meeting at Henry Wilcock's on the Kentish shore
(26th of 7 mo.), four justices of the peace, the high sheriff of Delaware as
well as the wife of Fox's patient, were at the meeting at 'x' (27th of 7 mo.),
while at the large general meeting which next followed (3rd–7th of 8 mo.,
probably at Betty's Cove or Thirdhaven) there was a judge and his wife
(perhaps the beneficiaries of Fox's cure) and another judge's wife (perhaps
the convert of 22nd of 7 mo.) and eight justices of the peace. But the
particular beneficiary of Fox's miracle he describes as being both a judge
and one of the Assembly.

Now there were in the Maryland Assembly as constituted and prorogued
by adjournments from 1671 to 1675 four representatives from Talbot
County. There were fourteen persons at the same time in the same county
who had commissions of Justice of the Peace (issued 17 December 1670),
but of these the 'Justices of the Quorum' or men who were authorized to
preside at the court were again only four. There are only two names that
occur alike both among the four Assemblymen and among the four judges—
Richard Woolman and Philemon Lloyd (Loyd, Floyd). It is probable that
Fox's description limits us to these two men. Both of them lived on Miles
River within the general area suggested by the identifiable details of the
context. Almost exactly contemporary indication of their residence is found
in the names 'Loyds Cr' and 'Woolmans Cr' right next to each other on
Augustin Herman's map of Maryland and Virginia (1674). The following are
the facts about each of them, derived principally from O. Tilghman's
History of Talbot County, Maryland, 1661–1861 (2 vols. Baltimore, 1905).

Colonel Philemon Lloyd lived at Wye House, which was near Doncaster,
an ancient town on Miles River near Bruff's Island, *alias* Crouch's Island.
His father was Edward Lloyd, the Puritan who came to Virginia about
1650, acquired title to the Wye House plantation in 1658, returned to
England in 1668, lived in London and married again, and when he died
(will dated 11 March 1695) devised Wye House to his son Philemon's son
Edward. The first wife of Edward Lloyd and mother of Philemon was Alice
Crouch. Philemon married Henrietta Maria, daughter of Captain James and
Anna Neale, and wealthy widow of Richard Bennett of Bennett's Point.
They had three sons and seven daughters before Philemon Lloyd died on
22 June 1685 in the 39th year of his age (Tilghman, op. cit. vol. I, pp. 146–55;
vol. II, pp. 38, 313 f.; and George A. Hanson, *Old Kent: The Eastern Shore of
Maryland* (Baltimore, 1876), p. 28, where, however, it is said Philemon died
2 January 1698 and his wife 4 May 1697). As already indicated, he held
various offices: burgess or delegate to the General Assembly (1670/1–82),
speaker of the Lower House (1681), commissioner for a treaty with the
Iroquois Indians (1682) and Justice of the Quorum (1670–84/5).

Colonel Richard Woolman was a citizen of Anne Arundel County which he
represented in the Assembly in 1659. When Talbot County was formed in

a horse and went with her. And he was finely raised up, and after came to our meetings, and then I came 3 miles back to the house and the man being much refreshed when I left him.

II, 229 (Maryland, 27th of 7 mo. 1672)

11 *b*   I having been out of the nation [beyond the seas, and when I came into England to Bristol, I heard my mother* had been very sick* and she was very glad to hear

---

1661 he was its first and only burgess, and served in that office with others to 1675. He was one of the Justices (and of the Quorum) from 1662 to 1680. The latter date is about the time of his death. Information about his wife I have not found. His lands still bear the name of Woolman's (Tilghman, op. cit. vol. I, p. 233).

Between these two men it seems impossible to decide. It is not said by Fox that either the judge or his wife became a Friend, and therefore the fact that (Henrietta) Maria (Neale) (Bennett) Lloyd was an ardent Catholic and the patron of the local Catholic chapel is not an argument for deciding for Woolman. Lloyd himself, as his will shows, was equally committed to the Protestant faith. Like the woman in Fox's narrative, Madam Lloyd seems to have been an energetic and independent person.

Fox does say, however, that the Judge when he recovered came to meetings and apparently that he was seen by Fox 'not long after very well'. It is tempting to look for later references to him. Fox mentions, as already noted, a meeting in the neighbourhood that held five days the following week at which a judge and his wife were present, and when he returns to Talbot County the following spring, Fox mentions at Wye River a very precious meeting where the judge of that county and his wife were present and were very tender (1st of 2 mo. 1673). Fox landed at Bristol on 28th of 4 mo. 1673, and promptly gave instructions to Friends there to send to Maryland sixteen copies of the newly published folio volume of the works of Edward Burrough, as a token of his love to the great men that kindly received him (H. J. Cadbury, *Swarthmore Documents in America* (1940), pp. 85 f.). A somewhat longer list of these designated recipients (James Bowden, *History of Friends in America*, vol. I, p. 358) includes the following:

'The Judge at Wye River, to be left with Robert Harwoods.'
'The Judge that liveth near Henry Wilcox, in Maryland.'
'One Floyd, about Wye, in Maryland.'
The last-named is certainly Philemon Lloyd. Richard Woolman may be one of the others.

11 *b*   The text of this was once (like no. 10 *a*) in the hand of George Fox. A copy of the holograph made about 1840 and attested by A. R. Barclay is extant in Friends House (Portfolio 31–81). Another copy (Tricket MSS.) contains both this item and the next. See *J.F.H.S.* (1910), vol. VII, p. 79 and (1919), vol. XVI, p. 61. Another copy of both this and the next is at Liverpool in the Nicholson MSS., vol. XVI. It also is said to be 'taken

of me and it did raise her up. And from Bristol I came to London and she sent to me desiring once more to see me before she died. And I not being very well to travel, and this news I heard to London from her out of the country. And in 10th month 1673 I, going down through the country to see her and setting my wife and family toward Lancashire, was taken by one Parker called a justice from a Friend's house and sent to Worcester prison, and there kept about a month, and at the sessions there they put the oath to me as a snare knowing I could not swear.

And then I was moved to London from Worcester before the judges, and in she hearing that I was prisoned and coming down to see her might strike her to the heart and grieve her, and though I told the justices and judges the end of my travel, and these merciless judges and justices had neither mercy nor justice but sent me down again from London to Worcester.

And when I heard she was dead it struck me for I did in verity love her as ever one could a mother, for she was a good honest virtuous and a right natured woman. And when I had read the letter of her death it struck a great weight upon my spirit, and it was in a travail for a quarter of an hour, and there being people in the room saw some sudden travail upon me though they said nothing. And when my spirit had gotten through I saw her in the resurrection and the life everlastingly with me over all, and father in the flesh also. So these wicked justices God will judge who hindered me from visiting according to her] motherly and tender desire.

---

from a paper of his own handwriting and signed by himself'. Slight differences of wording suggest that it was copied independently.

On Mary Fox, see II, 450 f. Fox's arrest while intending to visit her is narrated in the *Journal*. His arrest took place 17 December 1673. The order sending him to London is dated 25 December. His mother was buried 7 January. Cf. *Friends' Quarterly Examiner*, 1938, vol. LXXII, pp. 149 f. Of his 'father in the flesh' Christopher Fox little is known. He evidently predeceased his wife. In 1652 George wrote an epistle (*Epistles*, 1698, no. 5) to his 'dear father and mother in the flesh'.

12 *a*   His mother* had a dead palsy* [and had little use of one side and she often did fall down and then could not help herself, and had been so many years. And George Fox came to see her, and at night she fell down, and he was moved to take her by the hand, and it immediately left her, and she arose and could] go about her business.

12 *b*   My dear friend, George Fox,
    who art a father...weakness*...from my childhood.
                         Margaret Greenway*

13 *a–b*   I went to a meeting at Kingston*...persecutors*...Lord did prevent them.

And there was a man sick*...Nottingham*...Darbyshire*...Yorkshire*...of God and his Truth.

13 *c*   In London Margaret Bateman*...sick*...and she was well.

---

12 *a*   The text of this is from the Tricket MSS. where this brief piece which alone contains any 'miracle' is a kind of endorsement or postscript to the preceding.

12 *b*   Margaret Greenway has not been identified. Men with this surname appear to have suffered as Friends in many counties of England (Besse, *Suff.*, indexes). In 1659 a Margaret Greenway is the last name in the list of women from London and Southwark who protested against tithes (*These Several Papers*, p. 58).

13 *a–b*   Two endings and two beginnings show that the compiler of the index here has run together two items in the 'Book of Miracles'. In his later life Fox often visited the Rous family at Kingston-on-Thames. He often attended meeting there, and mentions the absence of actual molestation (III, 78, 87, 196). Probably some escape from persecutors in this period was narrated.

The other item evidently referred to an individual cure, but the county names suggest that it included some generalization, perhaps like that for 1655 in I, 195 f.: 'And from thence [Baddesley in Warwickshire] I passed into Nottinghamshire and had large meetings there and so into Darbyshire where the Lord's power came over all...and great miracles by the power of the Lord was done in many places by several...and Friends came out of Yorkshire to see us and was glad of the prosperity of Truth.'

13 *c*   Margaret Bateman of London signed the list of 7000 women who protested to Parliament against tithes in 1659 (*These Several Papers*, p. 56). Other references to her have not been found.

13 *d*   And there was a Scotch* woman...sick*...was made well.

13 *e*   And there was a merchant's wife*...sick*... arise and heal her.

14 *a*   And a widow woman* in Cheshire...not well*... and healed her.

14 *b*   And another woman* that kept her chamber*... the meeting to G.F.

14 *c*   In Somersetshire I came to a house...man*... pillows*...pillows were carried away.

14 *d*   In Wiltshire there was a woman*...not well*... the power of the Lord.

14 *e*   Thomas Briggs, Leonard Fell and J.P....distracted*...and her former health.

14 *f*   I came into Lancashire near...woman*...infirmities*...been well ever since.

14 *g*   And there was another woman*...bed*...to the glory of God.

15 *a*   And there was a Friend in London*...fever*... immediately well.

15 *b*   Mary Foster,* one of her...sick*...restored to health.

---

14 *c*   References to Fox in Somersetshire include a visit in 1659 (I, 348), in 1663, where the house he was in was searched about two o'clock in the night (II, 33), in 1668, including Minehead in late June (Ellwood (1694), p. 318), when he met a cheat, and Ilchester (II, 122–4). His host was often William Beaton of Podimore.

14 *e*   On Thomas Briggs and Leonard Fell, see I, 413 and I, 409, respectively. Both travelled widely in the spreading of Quakerism. If we knew at what times they travelled together, we might be able to identify both this occasion and a third person present whose initials are J.P. (James Parke?; John Perrot?; James Parnell?). Possibly that person was Isaac Penington, one of the few associates mentioned by Briggs himself in *An Account of Some of the Travels and Sufferings of Thomas Briggs* (1685).

15 *b*   On Mary Foster of London, see III, 301. Fox visited her often, once on 22 December 1686 when she was sick. She died a few days later (III, 164, 165). In 1675 Mary Foster, widow, was an inmate of the house of

15 *c*   John Holman of Weymouth was sick*...earth in these ages.

16 *a*   And at Shrewsbury...John Jay*...neck* (broke) ...astonishment of the country.

And there a Friend that was with me went to try a horse and got on his back, and the horse ran and cast him on his head and broke his neck, as they called it. And the people took him up dead, and carried him a good way and laid him on a tree. And I came to him and felt on him and saw that he was dead. And as I was pitying his family and him for he was one that was to pass with me through the woods to Maryland that land journey. And I took him by the hair of his head and his head turned like a cloth, it was so loose. And I threw away my stick and gloves and took his head in both my hands, and set my knees against the tree and raised his head and I did perceive it was not broken out that ways. And I put my hand under his chin and behind his head and raised his head two or three times with all my strength and brought it in, and

---

Gerard Roberts (*A Christian-Testimony Born by the People of God* (1679), p. 17; Besse, *Suff.*, vol. I, p. 438, calls her his under-tenant). She is mentioned also in no. 63 *c*.

15 *c*   John Holman of Weymouth is mentioned as suffering persecution in 1660 by Besse, *Suff.*, vol. I, p. 168. A John Holman, eldest son of Arthur Holman (d. about 1656) of Weymouth married Eleanor Williams about 1638, became a merchant in Jamaica and 'died beyond seas' in May 1670 (*Somerset and Dorset Notes and Queries* (1929), vol. XIX, p. 222; cf. ibid. (1895), vol. IV, p. 308), but nothing is said about his being a Friend.

16 *a*   For John Jay or Gay, see II, 437, where variant accounts of his accident and recovery may be seen. He is mentioned by Fox in a letter to Margaret Fox, 17th of 3 mo. 1674, of which he was the bearer (*Annual Catalogue*, 17, 138 F). According to Ellwood (1694), p. 368; (1891), vol. II, p. 172, he was a planter of Barbados. Fines levied upon him in Barbados in 1669 and 1674 are mentioned by Besse, *Suff.*, vol. II, pp. 284, 289. There was also a John Gay of Dublin who suffered in Ireland in 1660 and 1670 (Besse, *Suff.*, vol. II, pp. 465, 478). Fox's American companion died in Dublin in 1674. His will dated 20 April 1672, when he planned to leave Barbados, but not proved until 1679 gives further details of his family and possessions. He left a wife and a daughter both named Hannah, and a son Joseph. His home was in the parish of St Joseph in the Island, but both he and his wife had relations in England who are beneficiaries of the will.

The Bodleian MS. says the accident occurred at Porback near Shrewsbury. A still earlier version (Bristol MSS. v, 37 ff.) omits the words 'and broke his

I did perceive his neck began to be stiff. And then he began to rattle and after to breathe. And the people was amazed, and I bid them have a good heart and carry him into the house, and then they set him by the fire, and I bid them get him some warm things and get him to bed.

So after he had been in the house awhile he began to speak and did not know where he had been. And the next day we passed, and he with us pretty well, about 16 miles to a meeting at Middletown, and many hundreds of miles afterwards.

II, 226 *f* (Shrewsbury, New Jersey, 7 mo. 1672)

16 *b* There was a young woman*... toothache*... and went her ways.

17 In the days of Oliver Cromwell* he had a daughter ...sick*...and did get her mind.

And another time her they called the Lady Claypoole was very sick and troubled in mind and nothing could comfort her and I was

---

neck as they say' near the beginning, and omits at the end, 'and many hundreds of miles afterwards'. A modern surgical view of the episode is given by Dr Bedford Pierce in *J.F.H.S.* (1917), vol. XIV, p. 84. Elisha Kirk, a travelling Friend, in 1786 claims to have visited the house into which Jay was carried, then occupied by William Parker, and to have seen 'the log on which George Fox laid Jay, yet lying there with no more virtue than any other log' (Comly, *Miscellany*, vol. VI, p. 36).

17 Fox continues his narrative as follows: 'And many Friends got copies of that paper both in England and Ireland and read it to distracted people and it settled several of their minds and they did great service with it both in England and Ireland: which paper is in the book of my papers at London.' The 'book of papers' was probably one now lost, called N by the cataloguer. The paper to Lady Claypole occurred there on p. 25. Many of the originals from which N was composed are extant in the Swarthmore MSS. This one is now numbered VII. 123 in that collection. Its unedited text is the basis of the transcript here given. A volume (called by the cataloguer X), formerly owned by an Irish Friend, Lucretia Cook, is extant and contains this paper on p. 407. It was printed *in extenso* by Ellwood (1694, pp. 189 f.; 1891, I, 432 ff.). As the next two pages of the 'Book of Miracles' (18 and 19) contained apparently no other entries, one may conjecture that the full text of this letter was included at this point. Indeed, in the main body of the *Annual Catalogue*, 3, 79 D, this paper is listed as appearing not only in 189 Jo, 25 N, 407 X, but also in 17 0.

The paragraph quoted is included in the MS. *Journal* between the two references to Oliver Cromwell in 1658, the year of her death, but as it begins simply 'and another time', the date is uncertain. Had Ellwood any real moved of the Lord to write a paper and sent it to her to be read unto her and she said it settled and stayed her mind for the present.   I, 327 f.

17–19.

Friend,

Be still and cool in thy own mind and spirit from thy own thoughts, and then thou wilt feel the principle of God to turn thy mind to the Lord God, whereby thou wilt receive this strength and power from whence life comes to allay all tempests against blusterings and storms. That is it which moulds up into patience, into innocency, into soberness, into stillness, into stayedness, into quietness up to God with his power. Therefore mind,—that is the word of the Lord God unto thee,—that the authority and thy faith in that to work down, for that is it which keeps peace, and brings up the witness in thee that hath been transgressed, to feel after God who is a god of order and peace with his power and life. When transgression of the life of God in the particular the mind flies up in the air, and the creature is led into the night, and nature goes out of his course, and an old garment goes on, and an uppermost clothing, and nature leads out of his course, and so it comes to be all of a fire in the transgression, and that defaceth the glory of the first body. Therefore be still a while from thy own thoughts, searching, seeking, desires, imaginations and be stayed in the principle of God in thee to stay thy mind upon God, up to God,

---

authority for substituting 'about this time'? Her death on 6 August 1658 was preceded by a long weakness and illness, during which some occasional improvements were noted. It is probable that Fox's letter was written in July of that year, though she was also ill in earlier years. The nature of her final malady is not known, but it involved severe internal physical pain. It baffled the doctors and led friends to suggest remedies reputed to have worked miraculous cures. But it had the attention of the whole nation, since the Protector himself was absorbed with anxiety for his favourite daughter and was hastened to his own death by hers.

On Elizabeth Cromwell (1629–58), second daughter of Oliver Cromwell, and married in 1646 to John (later Lord) Claypoole (or Claypole), see I, 457, and beside the works there mentioned especially James Waylen, *The House of Cromwell* (rev. ed. 1897), ch. IX, and Robert W. Ramsey, *Studies in Cromwell's Family Circle and Other Papers* (1930), ch. I. At least two sons and two daughters are known, but none left issue. The 'Book of Miracles' mentions also her Quaker brother-in-law and his wife, James and Eleanor Claypole (nos. 75 *b*, 63 *e*).

VIII. Lady Elizabeth Claypole

From a miniature by Samuel Cooper at Windsor Castle.
By gracious permission of H.M. THE KING

and thou wilt find strength from him, and be a present help in time of trouble in need, and to be a god at hand, and it will keep thee humble, being come to the principle of God, which hath been transgressed, which humble God will teach in his way, which is peace and such he doth exalt. And now as the principle of God in thee hath been transgressed, come to it, to keep thy mind down low up to the Lord God, and deny thyself, and from thy own will, that is the earthly, thou must be kept. Then thou wilt feel the power of God that will bring nature into his course, and to see the glory of the first body, and there the wisdom of God will be received, which is Christ, by which all things was made and created, in which wisdom to be preserved and ordered to God's glory. There thou wilt come to receive and feel the physician of value which clothes people in their right mind whereby they may serve God and do his will.

For all distractions, distempers, unruliness, confusion, is in the transgression, which transgression must be brought down, before the principle that hath been transgressed be lifted up, whereby the mind may be seasoned and still'd, and a right understanding of the Lord, whereby his blessing enters and is felt over all that is contrary with the power of the Lord God which gives dominion, which awakens the principle of God within, which gives a feeling after God. Therefore keep in the fear of the Lord God. That is the word of the Lord unto thee, for all these things happeneth to thee for thy good, and your good, to make you to know your own strength and means, and to know the Lord's strength and power. Trust in him therefore. Let the time be sufficient that is past, who in anything hath been lifted up in transgression out of the power of the Lord, for he can bring down and abase the mighty ones and lay them in the dust of the earth. Therefore all keep low in his fear, that thereby you may receive the secret of God and his wisdom, and know the shadow of the Almighty, and sit under it in all tempests and storms and heats, for God is a god at hand, and the Most High, he rules in the children of men. So then this is the word of the Lord God unto you all, what the Light doth make manifest and discover temptations, confusion, distractions, distempers. Do not look at the temptations, confusions, corruptions, but at the Light that discovers them, that makes them manifest, and with the same Light you will feel over them, to receive power to stand against them, which Light discovers. The same Light that lets you see sin and transgression will let you see the covenant of God which blots out the sin and transgression, which gives victory and dominion over it and brings into covenant with God. For looking down at sin and corruption and distraction, you are swallowed up in it, but looking at the Light that discovers them you will see over them. That will give victory, and you will find grace and strength, and there is the first step of peace, that will bring salvation, and see to the beginning and the glory that was with the Father before the world began, and so come to know the seed of God which is heir of the promise of God and the world which hath no end unto the power of an endless life, which power of God is immortal, which brings up the soul which is immortal up to the immortal God in whom it doth rejoice. So in the name and power of the Lord Jesus strengthen thee.   G.F.

20   Ellis H[ookes],
I did write a few . . . girl* . . . infirmity* . . . loving friend
                                                    Brian Sixmith

21 *a*   And in Enemessy in Maryland* . . . moping* . . . miles, in the year 1673.

And there was a woman at Enemessy which had been many years in trouble and would sometimes sit moping near 2 months together and hardly speak nor mind anything. So I was moved to go to her and tell her that salvation was come to her house, and did speak

---

20   On Ellis Hookes, see II, 402, and more fully *J.F.H.S.* (1903), vol. I, pp. 12–22. As clerk of the Friends' Chamber in London he was perhaps collector of miracle material, as he was of replies to other questionnaires. Cf. *Extracts from State Papers*, p. 154. He died in 1681.

Bryan (Brewen, Bruan) Sixmith, with his wife Hester (d. 1686), lived at Warrington where he died in 1679. See Smith, *Catalogue*, vol. II, p. 578. But earlier he was a draper in High Street, next the Golden Lion, in Wrexham. See A. N. Palmer, *A History of the Older Nonconformity of Wrexham* (1888), p. 123. He was in frequent trouble with the authorities in that area in 1660 (Besse, *Suff.*, vol. I, p. 744), in 1661 (ibid. p. 748), in 1663 (Palmer, loc. cit.), in 1664 (*Extracts from State Papers*, p. 229), and in 1665 (*Baptist Historical Society Transactions* (1917), vol. V, p. 162). Two children predeceased him, Martha in 1674 and William in 1677. The latter was the subject of a memoir by his father (*Some Fruits brought forth through a Tender Branch*) and of one in *Piety Promoted*.

21 *a*   Annemessex is in Somerset County, Maryland, and became the site of a Friends' Meeting on the eastern shore. See for its early history Clayton Torrence, *Old Somerset on the Eastern Shore of Maryland* (Richmond, Virginia, 1935), pp. 85–94. In the same book will be found careful

other words to her and for her. And that hour she mended and passed up and down with us to meetings and is well, blessed be the Lord. II, 243 (Maryland, 3rd of 1 mo. 1673)

21 *b* In Yorkshire Gervase Benson* one of his... sick*...and she was healed.

21 *c* And in Berkshire* there was a w[oman]... ulcer*...and in the year 1673.

21 *d* And there was a distracted woman*...it was in Essex.

21 *e* And there came a man* unto...sick*...and was well. 1673.

22 *a* Rebekah Travers* her maid had the...ague*... before half a year.

---

identifications of persons and places in the context of this passage of Fox's *Journal*.

This narrative is apparently of the same event as 70 *a*. In this instance as in others (nos. 16 *a*, 75 *a*), the distance which the recovered patient travelled was cited at the end as proof of cure. No substantial difference from the text printed above is offered in Ellwood's edition (1694), p. 381; (1891), vol. II, p. 192, where the place is called Anamessy or Anamessic respectively, or in the earlier MS. *Journal* in the Bodleian or Bristol MSS.

21 *b* On Gervase Benson, see I, 403. He is the same as Justice Benson mentioned in no. 60 *d*, but whether two miracles were related of him, or one related twice does not appear. His home was near Sedbergh, Yorks. Considerable information about him will be found in *F.P.T.*, pp. 250–2. The fragmentary text suggests that one of his maids or daughters was the subject. Only one daughter, Catherine, born in 1650, appears in the Friends' registers.

21 *c* If this item combined Fox with both the county and the year mentioned, one recalls that he landed in Bristol from America on 28 June 1673, and stayed to the fair a month later. Among the many places which he visited after that and before his arrest in mid-December was Reading in Berkshire. For other references to an ulcer or ulcers, see nos. 45 *a*, 66 *a* and 70 *b* (with note). In all instances the afflicted persons were women.

21 *d* Compare nos. 28 *b–c* with its 'distracted' person in Essex.

22 *a* On Rebecca Travers, a prominent Friend of London, see III, 312 f. Fox was a frequent visitor at her house. An example of her warm affection for Fox (and of her unorthodox spelling) may be seen in my *Swarthmore Documents in America* (1940), pp. 74 ff.

22 *b*   And a young woman* her mother...had made her well.

22 *c*   And another young woman* was...small pox*... of God was made well

22 *d*   My very dear Friend,
George Fox,
I received...Thy dear Friend
Charles Lloyd*

24 *a*   In London* in Oliver's days...reprobate*... sick*...before I came away.

24 *b*   And there came one 10 miles...child*...sick*... was well. In the year 1673.

24 *c*   I went to a Friend's house...child*...sick*... praised be the Lord. In 1674.

24 *d*   And there was a young woman...London*... sick*...that raised her up. 1674.

25   As I was passing over the sea...Ireland*...seen in the vision*.

---

22 *d*   On Charles Lloyd, Jr. (1637–98) of Dolobran, Montgomeryshire, see II, 407; III, 323. Letters by him to his daughter and a life of him by his daughter are in MS. at Friends' House, London.

25   There are other visions included among the miracles. A vision appeared to Fox at Bandon in Ireland of a very ugly visaged man black and dark. This he understood to be an intimation that he must ride through the city of Cork, which he did (II, 139 f.). But no vision is recorded precisely at the time of his passing from England over the sea to Ireland.

Probably the passage here referred to was his voyage in *The Society of Bristol* from Virginia *over the sea* to Bristol in 1673, during the Dutch War. The reports that Dutch men-of-war had taken thirteen British ships near New York and that several had been taken about Scilly and the coasts of *Ireland* gave grounds for fears not only to the captain and men but to the passengers. At least three accounts are preserved written by Fox of a vision he had of 'two ships to the Westward that should make towards us but should do us no hurt'. They saw one on the 31st of 4th month at the Capes of Virginia, another three or four days later to their westward. Fox recognized them as those which he had *seen in the vision*. They saw no more ships until they reached Bristol harbour. Two accounts are printed in II, 247 f., 253 f.

26 *a*   And there was another maid* had sore lips*...
that brought her to G.F.

26 *b*   And G.F. came to a meeting...woman*...
ague*...fever*...and G.F. stayed her.

26 *c*   Another time there was a woman*...dumb*...
was a great miracle.

26 *d*   And G.F. came into an house...King's evil*...
it left the child*.

26 *e*   A woman* had a great pain* in her head*...pain
went away.

26 *f*   And there was another woman*...sick*...was
raised up.

27 *a*   And there was a woman that...child*...King's-
evil*...that time was healed.

And there was a woman brought her daughter to show me how
well she was, which had had the King's evil. For when I was there
before she desired me to lay my hands on her and pray for her,
which I did and it was immediately made well

II, 310 (Cossell, 4 mo. 1675)

27 *b*   My dear Friend.
        George Fox,
           My little...child*...died*...love to thee.
                                        Clare Hartas

---

26 *d*   Other cases of King's evil are mentioned in nos. 27 *a*, 56 *g*, 61 *a*.

27 *a*   Cossell is not certainly identified—perhaps a Coleshill in Warwickshire. Cf. II, 268. There is a Cossal in Notts, and a Coleshill in Bucks and one
in Herts. It is mentioned here on Fox's journey from London to Swarthmore
as a stop between Coventry and Whitechurch. The narrative quoted above
was not dictated at first in the *Journal*, but was early added to the manuscript. On what previous occasion Fox had been there the *Journal* does not
indicate. A fuller journal might have mentioned the episode twice, once
when the girl was first visited and once on this later occasion. Possibly in
the 'Book of Miracles' this was done and we have here the first reference,
and in no. 56 *g* we have the second, 'G.F. coming from London', etc.

With the closing phrase here, compare that cited from Fox's *Journal* under
no. 8, p. 101: 'the woman was healed that time'.

27 *b*   Clare Hartas and her husband George Hartas of Ulrome (Olrome,
Oreham, Oram) were among the firstfruits of the ministry of William

117

28 *a*   There was a youth, a golds[mith's]...London*...
ague*...which was in the year 1674.

28 *b–c*   G.F. came into Essex...distracted*...

And since her boy* was sick...ague*...fever*...had it
no more...to the praise of God. 1680

31 *a*   There was a man sick*...according to his word.

31 *b*   He came into Leicestershire* where...sick*...
turn his servant away.

At Twycross in Leicestershire I was moved to go to see a great
man that was sick, and after I had spoke to him in his bed, and the
power of the Lord entered him, that he was loving and tender.
And I left him and came down among the family in the house
and spake a few words to the people that they should fear the
Lord and repent and prize their time and the like words.

And there came one of his servants with a naked sword and run
at me ere I was aware of him and set it to my side, and there held

---

Dewsbury in Yorkshire in 1652 (*F.P.T.* p. 297). They had at least ten
children who survived the father's death in 1670. See I, 401.

28 *a*   At least one Quaker goldsmith in London is known, Humphrey
Bache or Bates, whose house at the Sign of the Snail in Tower Street, was
one of the early meeting places of Friends, 'Snail Meeting'. As he died in
1662 he is not probably the goldsmith whose son or apprentice (?) was
mentioned here, nor indeed is there any presumption that the goldsmith was
a Friend.

28 *b–c*   Two incidents have been combined by the cataloguer as is shown
by the occurrence of two different endings. With the distracted person in
Essex compare no. 21 *d*.

31 *b*   The passage in the 'Book of Miracles' evidently included the double
episode of the sick master and the violent servant, as in the passage cited
from the *Short Journal*. The account in Ellwood (1694, p. 30; 1891, I, 49)
differs considerably from this in wording. That was, however, doubtless
derived from the early pages of the Spence MS. which are now lost. For the
latter includes a cross-reference to this event in 1662: 'And afore we came
into Warwickshire at a place called Twycross where that great man whom
the Lord God had raised up from his sickness whose man came with a drawn
sword to have done me a mischief; he and his wife came to see me.' (II, 18 f.;
cf. Ellwood, 1694, p. 258; 1891, I, 536.) Here Ellwood gives the date of the
first visit as 1649. Croese writes (*General History*, Engl. tr. 1696, p. 28):
'Fox did likewise boast that he cured a certain man in a village called
Trikossio in Leicestershire, after he had been given over by the physicians,
only by uttering some few words to him, and stretching forth his hand to

it, and I looked up at him in his face and said to him, 'Alack for thee, it's no more to me than a straw,' and then he went away in a rage, with threatening words, and I passed away.

And the power of the Lord came over all, and his master mended according to my belief and faith that I had seen before, and he turned this man away that had run at me with the sword.

III, 15 (1649)

31 *c* Here follows a r...was given to G. Fox*.

32 *a* For it was shewed unto G.F....priests*... without the equity.

While I was there, the Lord opened to me three things relating to those three great professions in the world, Physick, Divinity (so

---

heaven.' The last phrase may be due to Croese's imagination, the spelling of the village is due to the Latin here translated, but the phrase 'given over by the physicians' is apparently due to Ellwood's *Journal*.

The following variant account is taken from an unprinted MS. in Friends' House, London (see *Annual Catalogue*, 121, 2 H):

'And one time George Fox went to one Noel's house, a gentleman in Leicestershire, to visit him, he being sick. And the man and his wife took it very kindly, and he did recover.

'And as he came down the stairs, one of his serving men was so full of rage that he ran at him with his naked rapier, and set it to his side. And George Fox lifted up his eyes upon him, and said, "Alas, poor creature! What wilt thou do with thy carnal weapon?" and said unto him it was no more to him than a straw. But after his master heard of it, he turned him away.'

This account gives the man's name as Noell (or Noel or Nowell). This does not, however, quite identify him. The Noel family of Leicestershire was long connected with Kirkby Malory, which is not near Twycross. At Sibson, however, which is a neighbouring village to Twycross lived Edward Noel, a member of the Kirkby Malory family, and there was a branch of the family at Wellsborough, a hamlet of Sibson, in the seventeenth century. Edward Noel was rector of Sibson between 1642 and 1648 and again sometime later. At the time of this episode he was dispossessed, and he may have been living at Twycross, as is suggested by a slightly later entry in the Parish Register of Twycross: 'Elizabeth Noel, daughter of Edward and Elizabeth, buried 29 Dec. 1652.' (Information from Miss Eleanor Swift, Keeper of the Archives, City of Leicester Museum.)

31 *c* What remains of this item and of the next does not resemble the typical material in the 'Book of Miracles'. Possibly this contained an opening given to Fox, like no. 32 *a*, or was even the introduction to that. The surviving 'r' could stand for 'revelation' or for 'relation'.

32 *a* The identification of this item with the incident in the *Journal* may be questioned. The surviving words 'shewed', 'priests' and 'without the

called) and Law. And he showed me that the physicians and doctors of physic were out of the Wisdom of God, by which the Creatures were made; and so knew not the virtues of the Creatures, because they were out of the word of Wisdom, by which they were made. And he showed me, that the priests were out of the true faith, which Christ is the author of, the faith which purifies and gives victory and brings people to have access to God, by which they please God; which mystery of faith is held in a pure conscience. He showed me also that the lawyers were out of the equity and out of the true justice, and out of the law of God, which went over the first transgression and over all sin and answered the Spirit of God that was grieved and transgressed in man. And that these three, the physicians, the priests and the lawyers ruled the world out of the wisdom, out of the faith, and out of the equity and law of God; the one pretending the cure of the body, the other the cure of the soul, and the third the property of the people. But I saw they were all out, out of the Wisdom, out of the faith, out of the equity and perfect law of God.

> Ellwood, *Journal*, 1694, 18; 1891, I, 29
> (Clauson in the Vale of Beavor,
> Leicestershire, 1648)

---

equity' will, however, be seen to fit the passage in Ellwood who may well have found in the pages of the MS. *Journal* that are now lost the substance of the passage as he gives it. Some slight confirmation may be found in the fact that the episodes before and after this in the 'Book of Miracles' belong also to the earliest years. There were other visions and openings in the 'Book of Miracles', and the part of this one dealing with the physicians may have been responsible for its being included.

A reference to the same incident showing the use of the same general language may be quoted from his remarks at Yearly Meeting in London in 1674, not many months from the probable date at which he wrote the *Journal* passage. I quote from the Richardson MSS. p. 94 (typescript copy, p. 227; see *Annual Catalogue*, 17, 36 F and pp. 24 f.): 'Now as to the priests I did not look upon them as the only false prophets for they were made up of thick darkness itself, they lay all without the faith of God, never came to it; and the physicians without the wisdom of God, and the lawyers without equity in the Fall, and that they should never do us much hurt. These things I saw before ever I appeared abroad in the Lord's work.'

The parallel discomfiture of priests and physicians is suggested by a letter from Morgan Watkins to Mary Penington at the time of the Great Plague. Writing as a prisoner from the Gate House, London, 18 September 1665, he says: 'Many doctors of physic who made a great ado about stopping the disease are dead, and several priests.' Barclay, *Letters, &c. of Early Friends* (1841) p. 149.

32 b There was a woman in Nottinghamshire*...
distracted*...the woman recovered.

And coming to Mansfield Woodhouse there was a distracted
woman under a doctor's hand, with her hair loose all about her
ears; and he was about to let her blood, she being first bound, and
many people being about her, holding her by violence, but he could
get no blood from her. And I desired them to unbind her and let
her alone, for they could not touch the spirit in her by which she
was tormented. So they did unbind her. And I was moved to
speak to her and in the name of the Lord to bid her be quiet and
still. And she was so. And the Lord's power settled her mind and
she mended; and afterwards received the Truth and continued in
it to her death. And the Lord's name was honoured to whom the
glory of all his works belongs.

> Ellwood, *Journal* (1694), pp. 27 f.; (1891), ɪ, 45
> (Mansfield Woodhouse in Nottingham-
> shire, 1649)

32 c And also in Leicestershire* they said...dis-
tracted*...she was recovered.

33 a When G.F. was cast...Nottingham*...been possessed*. 1650...in the year 1650.

When I was a prisoner in the same place there came a woman to
me to the prison and two with her and said that she had been
possessed two and thirty years. And the priests had kept her and
had kept fasting days about her and could not do her any good.
And she said the Lord said unto her, 'Arise for I have a sanctified
people. Haste, and go to them, for thy redemption draweth nigh.'
And when I came out of prison I bade Friends have her to
Mansfield. And at that time our meetings were disturbed by wild

---

32 b   For the possible identity of this with no. 33 a, see the note to that.

33 a   This narrative did not occur in Ellwood and presumably not in the
lost part of the Spence MSS. The cure took place, however, after Fox's
release from Nottingham gaol as did that in no. 32 b, and it is natural that
Norman Penney (ɪɪɪ, 275) suggests that this story of the possessed woman
at Nottingham, Mansfield and Skegby may be reminiscent of the same
event as is related of a distracted woman at Mansfield Woodhouse. If,
however, they are correctly identified with paragraphs in the 'Book of
Miracles' as nearly in sequence as nos. 32 b and 33 a respectively, they are

people, and both them and the professors and priests said that we were false prophets and deceivers and that there was witchcraft amongst us. And the poor woman would make such a noise in roaring and sometimes lying along upon her belly upon the ground and with her spirit and roaring and voice, and would set all Friends in a heat and sweat. And I said, 'All Friends keep to your own, lest that which is in her get into you.' And so she affrighted the world from our meetings. And then they said if that were cast out of her while she was with us, and were made well, then they would say that we were of God. This said the world, and I had said before that she should be set free.

And then it was upon me that we should have a meeting at Skegby at Elizabeth Hooton's house, when we had her there. And there were many Friends almost overcome by her with the stink that came out of her, roaring and tumbling on the ground. And the same day she was worse than ever she was, and then another day we met about her, and about the first hour the life rose in Friends, and said it was done and she rose up and her countenance changed and became white and before it was wan and earthly. And she sat down at my thigh as I was sitting and lift up her hands and said, 'Ten thousand praise the Lord', and did not know where she was, and so she was well.

And we kept her about a fortnight in the sight of the world and she wrought and did things, and then we sent her away to her friends. And then the world's professors, priests and teachers never could call us any more false prophets, deceivers, or witches after, but it did a great deal of good in the country among people in relation to the Truth, and to the stopping the mouths of the world and their slanderous aspersions.

III, 2 f. (Nottingham and Mansfield Woodhouse, 1649)

---

not likely to be doublets. For Fox 'possessed' and 'distracted' are not quite interchangeable.

Fox has, however, another account of this event beside the one printed here from the *Short Journal*. It differs little from this one though written twenty-five years later (*How the Lord by His Power and Spirit*, etc.).

From that source the story came to Gerard Croese, *General History* (Engl. tr. 1696), pp. 27 f., and from there to F. Bugg, *A Brief History of Quakerism* (1697), p. 69. Also in his testimony to Elizabeth Hooton (see above, p. 60) Fox probably refers to this event. The fact that the next entry in the 'Book of Miracles' began two pages later suggests that this entry was given there with a fullness commensurate to the fullness of his other accounts of it.

35 *a*   And after G.F. was cast...Derby*...child-bed*...they recovered.
...the woman was delivered.

35 *b*   He came to William Dewsbury's* house... leg*...hath spoken of it. About 1652.

35 *c*   And he came to a place...boy*...ague* got over his ague.

36 *a*   At Cartmel there was a man...ague*...fever*... he came in again.

36 *b*   There was a maid that was distracted*...made her well.

37 *a*   And then he came to C...child*...sick*... prisoner and at his house.

37 *b*   And there came a woman...distracted*...she was now, etc.

37 *c*   And there came another...distracted*...afterward recovered.

---

35 *a*   The Derby imprisonment of Fox was 1650–1. The indexer as elsewhere has varied in his determining what words to quote as the final words of this piece.

35 *b*   Probably this event is that related by Dewsbury. See above, p. 59. The date and the reference to a leg are appropriate. On Dewsbury, see I, 399. In 1655 his home was at Wakefield in Yorkshire, but in 1652 he probably lived still at his birthplace, Allerthorpe, Yorks. See Edward Smith, *Life of William Dewsbury*, 1836, p. 58.

36 *a*   Cartmel, across one arm of the bay from Swarthmore, was visited by Fox in 1652, 1653, 1663 and probably at other times. It was the home of John Braithwaite, James Taylor and other Friends, and also for a time of priest Philip Bennet. The account of the first publishers of 'Truth' there was first published in *J.F.H.S.* (1934), vol. XXXI, pp. 11 f.
   The closing words indicate that the man of this narrative 'ran out' from Friends (i.e. became a renegade), but that later he came in again. This was the experience of Richard Myers and James Milner both of whom lived at Baycliff near Swarthmore (I, 107; cf. I, 200; II, 111, etc.).

36 *b*   The four accounts of 'distracted' persons on pp. 36 and 37 of the 'Book of Miracles' show arrangement by association of ideas.

37 *d*   There was one Anthony Stubbs*...distracted*... according to his faith.

38 *a*   And G.F. came to Thomas Hunter*...sick*... great while afterward.

38 *b*   He came another time into Bishoprick*...to eat*...dumb*...remained a good Friend.

And in Bishopric whilst I was there they brought a woman tied behind a man that could neither eat nor speak and had been so a great while. And they brought her into the house to me at Anthony Pearson's. And I was moved of the Lord God to speak to her, that she ate and spake and was well, and got up behind her husband without any help and went away well.

I, 140 (Rampshaw Hall, County Durham, 1653)

38 *c*   Then after he came to...John Fallowfield*... consumption*...well to his father.

39   And also there was another woman*...sick*... ague*...fever*...from her infirmity.

39–40   And so the second day George coming... woman*...sick*...but three or four days. ...are recovered.

---

37 *d*   Anthony Stubbs is a name not known to occur elsewhere in Quaker records.

38 *a*   A Thomas Hunter wrote from Holeraw (now called Hole Row) in Northumberland to Fox 14th of 1 mo. 1653 (Swarthmore MSS. iv. 209). Distraint was made on Thomas Hunter in Cumberland in 1662 (Besse, *Suff.*, vol. I, p. 129). There is no way to tell whether either of them is the one mentioned here.

38 *b*   This with three other miracles printed in I, 140 f. was omitted by Ellwood, cf. 40. With the ending compare the ending of the first paragraph from Samuel Hooton quoted above, p. 9. There is a note on Anthony Pearson at I, 470.

38 *c*   John Fallowfield of Great Strickland is mentioned in various Quaker records (*F.P.T.* etc.). According to Norman Penney there was also a Cumberland man of this name (*Household Account Book*, p. 542). In Besse, op. cit. vol. I, p. 134, a man of this name is fined for meeting at Pardsley Crag in Cumberland.

39–40   The indexer found two endings to this piece. Though he did not include it under George Fox, I expect George means Fox.

40   And   also   at   that   time...boy*...crooked*...
scabbed*...meeting at that time.

And as I came out of Cumberland one time I came to Hawkshead
and lighted at a Friend's house, and there was young Margaret Fell
with me and William Caton. And it being a very cold season we
lighted and the lass made us a fire, her master and dame being gone
to the market. And there was a boy lying in the cradle which they
rocked, about eleven years old, and he was grown almost double
and I cast my eye upon the boy, and seeing he was dirty I bid the
lass wash his face and his hands and get him up and bring him unto
me.

So she brought him to me and I bid her take him and wash him
again for she had not washed him clean. Then I was moved of the
Lord God to lay my hands upon him and speak to him, and so bid
the lass take him again and put on his clothes, and after we passed
away.

And sometime after I called at the house and I met his mother
but did not light. 'Oh stay,' says she, 'and have a meeting at our
house for all the country is convinced by the great miracle that was
done by thee upon my son. For we had carried him to Wells and
the Bath and all the doctors had given him over. For his grand-
father and father feared he would have died and their name have
gone out, having but that son. But presently after you was gone,'
says she, 'we came home and found our son playing in the streets.'
Therefore, said she, all the country would come to hear if I would
come back and have a meeting there. And this was about three
years after that she told me of it, and he was grown to be a straight
full youth then; and so the Lord have the praise.

I, 140 f. (Hawkshead, Lancashire)

41 *a*   Then G.F. went into Yorkshire...boy*...sick*
...dying*...staring at him.

41 *b*   And when the meeting was done...child*...
sick*...astonishment to the people.

---

40   This with three other cures in I, 140 f. was omitted by Ellwood, cf.
no. 38 *b*. The date is not indicated, but it was obviously early, perhaps as
early as 1653, the year in which these four cures are interpolated in the
Spence MSS.

42 *a–b* Then G.F. came into Warw[ickshire]...headache*...arm*...faith she was well.

...Watkinson*...both of them were well.

42 *c* And so G.F. passed away...Storrs*...sick*...became an honest Friend

And from thence [Oram], [I passed] to Marmaduke Storr's where we had a large meeting at a constable's house on whom the Lord had wrought a great miracle, as in the book of miracles may be seen.   II, 106 (Owstwick, Yorks, 1666)

43 *a* And then some time after...Kent*...smallpox*...immediately recovered.

---

42 *a–b* The indexer has combined two episodes or confused two endings. George Watkinson, of Scotton, Yorkshire, former captain of the army and justice (I, 308) may be intended. On his bequests to Friends, see *Extracts from State Papers*, pp. 317, 330–2. A more conspicuous Friend was Morgan Watkins (I, 448), whose name is spelled Watkison in Fox's *Journal* (I, 274). Fox visited George Watkinson's house in Pontefract in 1657 (Ellwood, 1694, p. 281*; (1891), I, 416, a page missing from Spence MSS.). In the previous year when Fox and many others were in Launceston prison 'Captain Watkinson of Yorkshire being come down to see Friends interceded in their behalf' (Swarthmore MSS. I, 166, letter of Alexander Parker to Margaret Fell 19th of 6 mo. 1656). On his military history and dismissal see, beside I, 454, Davies and Firth, *Regimental History of Cromwell's Army* (1940), pp. 267, 272. Watkinson was a Captain of horse in Robert Lilburne's regiment which with seven other of Cromwell's regiments invaded Scotland in 1650. He is described by an associate as a person of great worth for conduct and valour, and it was he that gave the alarm when a picked detachment of Scots attacked them at Musselburgh on 31 July. On 26 October 1657 he was cashiered by Monck with Lieutenant Matthew Foster of Bradford's troop. According to Monck a certain Cornet Denham had been instrumental in making Watkinson a Quaker.

42 *c* On Marmaduke Storr, see I, 426. The reference to the 'Book of Miracles' in Spence MSS. was added after the first draft of the passage was written, but by Thomas Lower the same writer. It was omitted by Ellwood (1694, p. 307; 1891, II, 75). The index under 'sick' enters this item as on p. 62, under 'Storrs' as on p. 42. There is evidence that the latter is right.

43 *a* This and the following are indexed under 'Kent, County'. Fox was there several times, once as early as 1655. Attention may be called to the similarity of the endings in nos. 43 *a*, 43 *c*, 43 *d*, and 43 *e*.

43 b And in the same town there...Kent*...sick*...
for us to refresh us.

43 c G.F. came to London* and there...Martins*...
eye*...immediately it was well.

43 d And another time coming to London...Elizabeth
Trott*...smallpox*...presently recovered.

43 e And so he went to another...London*...dis-
tracted*...immediately she mended.

44 a And again he came into Y[orkshire]...child*...
diseased*...glad and rejoiced.

44 b G.F. came into Cornwall*...convulsion* fits away.

44 c And then he came d[own]...Cheshire*...knee*
...so she was well.

44 d And also there was...Pyott*...sick*...and said
he was well.

45 a And so he came to London*...ulcers*...head*
...to come nigh her.

45 b And there was another woman...London*...
sick*...spotted fever*...husband dressed furs.

46 And G.F. went to a meeting at Mile-End*...
Wapping*...troubled*...and serviceable to the Truth.

---

43 b I suspect that this narrative concludes with the patient offering re-
freshment to Fox and others, as in the Gospel story of Peter's wife's mother.

43 c Martins is probably by Quaker avoidance of 'Saint' a reference to
the well-known parish of St Martin's, London. Or it may be the surname
Martin which was borne by several Friends in London and elsewhere.

43 d Elizabeth Trott, widow, of London, not only gave her house on Pall
Mall as a meeting place but entertained Margaret Fell there when the latter
was in London (cf. I, 373; Swarthmore MSS. I, 170, 171, 172; A. R. Barclay,
MSS. 82) in 1660 or 1661. She was in Barbados in 1662 with her daughter
Abiah (Swarthmore MSS. III, 120) and died in 1666 or 1668, leaving her
daughter in care of Fox as a guardian. See I, 466; Beck and Ball, *London*,
pp. 240 f.

44 c Visits of Fox to Cheshire are mentioned in the *Journal* in 1657
(*bis*), 1660, 1667 and 1669.

44 d For Edward Pyott and his illnesses, see no. 49 b.

46 Mile End and Wapping are rarely mentioned in the *Journals* of Fox,
even in the *Itinerary Journals* of his later years about London. A Friend of

48   And from thence he went...Wellingborough*..
Ellington*...infirmity*...into stargazing, etc.

48–9   And also G.F. came into Hert[fordshire]...
Baptist*...dying*...done at Baldock.

And we was at a place called Baldock and I said to them 'Is
there nothing in this town, no profession?' And they told me there
was some Baptists and a Baptist woman. And John Rush went

Mile End was John Sellwood, brewer (III, 381). At Wapping lived two sisters,
Martha and Mary Meakins who married in 1678 William Dry and James
Strutt respectively (III, 341). In April 1687 Fox's *Diary* records that 'he
went to visit Martha Dry at Wapping who was not well...and visited old
Mary Strutt who was muddled in mind' (III, 171).

'Troubled' probably means troubled in mind, a term that may be
illustrated by the quotation from Fox's *Journal* given above under no. 17,
or (as a noun) by the title of a stout contemporary volume: '*A Discourse
concerning Trouble of Mind and the Disease of Melancholy.* By Timothy
Rogers, M.A. who was Long Afflicted with both' (London, 1691).

48   Ellington like Wellingborough may be a place-name. An identified
place is referred to thus on 24 March 1683, 'he went to visit a woman at
Ellington not well in her mind' (III, 90). There were Friends enough at
Ellington to have a monthly meeting there in the seventeenth century.
But a Francis Ellington of Wellingborough figures conspicuously under
Northamptonshire in Besse (cf. *Extracts from State Papers*, 9 f.) and *F.P.T.*,
and probably the 'Book of Miracles' refers to him or one of his family.
At his trial at Northampton in July 1655 Ellington implies that he had
served the Commonwealth in the wars and that for fifteen or sixteen years
he had been an employer in cording, spinning, dyeing and weaving of wool,
having 'imployed more poor people in work about wool, than any one man
in this Country [i.e. County] doth'. (Besse, *Abstract of Sufferings*, vol. I,
pp. 447 f.; so the *Works of William Dewsbery* (1689), p. 76.) The quarter
sessions records for that year are lacking, but those for 1657 include a recog-
nizance, an indictment for blasphemy, a jury list and sentence, and a com-
mitment for Francis Ellington, late of Wellingborough, upholsterer. See Joan
Wake, *Quarter Sessions Records of the County of Northampton* (Northamptonshire Record Society (1924), vol. I, nos. 273, 347, 488 and 491 [26]). His
writings are duly listed in Joseph Smith's *Descriptive Catalogue*. One refers
to the trial just mentioned. His *Christian Information concerning These Last
Times* (1664) is concerned to vindicate Quakerism not from prophecy but
from its fulfilment of prophecy not merely in the Scriptures but in William
Lilly's *Monarchy or No Monarchy* and in a book of Jacob Behmen bearing the
same title as his own but published in 1623.

48–9   On Thomas Baldock of Baldock, see I, 434. The account in the
Journal goes on to say that he and his wife became Friends and held large
meetings in their house. His wife and daughter were complained of for

IX. George Fox and the Baptist Woman

alongst with me to visit her and when we came there was a many people in the house that was tender about her. And they told me she was not a woman for this world and if I had anything to comfort her concerning the world to come I might.

So I was moved of the Lord God to speak to her and the Lord raised her up that she was well to the astonishment of the town and country. Her husband's name was Baldock of Baldock.

I, 199 (Baldock, Hertfordshire, 1655)

49 *a* And some had him to...Wellingborough*... fever*...of the people of God.

49 *b* And G.F. came to Bristol...Pyot*...fever*... ague*...of hundreds of people.

50 *a* And so G.F. went into...fever*...confounded the doctors.

50 *b* So G.F. came to one's h....fever*...praised God.

51 *a* G.F. came to a woman...leg*...and she mended.

51 *b* G.F. came to another place...issue* of blood*... Lord's power healed her.

---

attending meetings in 1675 (*Hertfordshire County Records* (1905), vol. I, p. 266). His own name appears as late as 1685 (ibid. (1930), vol. VI, see index). Cf. Besse, *Suff.*, vol. I, p. 242 (1661), p. 253 (1684).

49 *a* Wellingborough, see no. 48.

49 *b* On Edward Pyott, see I, 424. Other recoveries of Pyott from sickness are mentioned, e.g. above in no. 44 and in I, 204, where it is recorded that in 1655 while travelling with Fox at an inn at Totnes 'Edward Pyot was sick but the Lord's power healed him'. Again in 1656 at Launceston he was sick of a fever for thirteen days in Doomsdale (*West Answering North*, p. 40). In 1670 Pyott was in London very ill (Swarthmore MSS. I, 381; Webb, *Fells* (1886), pp. 279 f.).

This item in the 'Book of Miracles' probably dealt with the illness described in a letter written at Bristol on 28th of 5 month 1662 by John Stubbs to Margaret Fell a few days after Fox had arrived at Bristol: 'Edward was a dying man to all appearance when we came first to his house and George ordered him to take things and he was subject to him and now he is fine and well. His ague hath left him. The thing is much noised amongst Friends, he being so weak and no likelihood of his life' (II, 22). Ellwood (1694, p. 254; 1891, I, 528) in embodying this letter as Fox's own account omits among other phrases 'ordered him to take things and he was subject to him'.

52 *a*   And there was a woman...Lawson*...sick*...
she would recover.

52 *b*   G.F. went to another house...sick*...ague*...
fever*...this was in Redriff.

52 *c*   There was a woman...blind*...the child saw.

52 *d*   And many more of several diseases*...to set
down.

53 *a*   There was a young woman...fever*...she was
made well.

53 *b*   So G.F. passed a pretty...fever*...astonishing
of people.

53 *c*   And there was a man...sickness*...ague* any
more.

53 *d*   In Westmorland in a great m[eeting]...Myers*
...arm*...heard it and saw it.

And after I went to a meeting at Arnside where there was a many
people, and I was moved of the Lord to say to Richard Myers
amongst all the people, 'Prophet Myers, stand up upon thy legs,'
for he was sitting down. And he stood up and stretched out his arm
which had been lame a long time, and said, 'Be it known unto you
all people and to all nations that this day I am healed.'

And after the meeting was done his father and mother could
hardly believe it was made whole, and had him into an house and

---

52 *a*   Among Friends named Lawson the most conspicuous was Thomas
Lawson, a learned man and a botanist. See I, 408, and also p. 48 above.

52 *b*   Redriff is probably the popular spelling (and pronunciation) of
Rotherhithe, Surrey near London. Redriff is 'the name which it bears to this
day in the parlance of its waterside inhabitants'. (E. J. Beck, *Memorial to
serve for a History of the Parish of St Mary, Rotherhithe* (1907), p. 1.) The
place does not seem to be mentioned by name in Fox's *Journals*.

52 *c*   Another blind patient is mentioned in no. 58 *a*. Cf. no. 43 *c*.

52 *d*   This whole sentence or paragraph was probably a general reference
to several miracles. These summaries are characteristic. Cf. no. 54–5 below,
and II, 153: 'much might be written of these things'.

53 *d*   On Richard Myers, see I, 416. The account tells that he died about
nine months afterwards, in punishment as Fox thought for disobeying a
command of the Lord to go to York with a message.

took off his doublet, and then they saw it was true. And he came to Swarthmore meeting and there declared how the Lord had healed him. i, 107 f. (Arnside, Westmorland, 1653)

54–5 G.F. being then in Leicester...a cold*... dying*...too great a volume.

55 *a* And G.F. when he was prisoner* at L^r...sick* of a fever*.

55 *b* And there was one Daniel Baker*...crutch*... twenty years since.

54–5 For the manner of expression at the end compare above p. 38 and iii, 47: 'Many miraculous deliverances I had which would make a great volume if they should be declared.' Cf. no. 52 *d*.

55 *a* The abbreviation L^r may be resolved so as to place this event during Fox's imprisonment at Leicester 1662 or during that at Lancaster, 1664–5. For the latter compare no. 56 *a*, for the former perhaps no. 54–5.

55 *b* Daniel Baker's cure from lameness (crutches) was the subject also of no. 65 *a-b* and perhaps of no. 60 *a*. Whenever mentioned it is described as of long standing at the time of writing.

On Daniel Baker, see ii, 380, to which much more information could be added not only from Quaker sources, but from the State Papers in the Public Record Office which enable us to follow his career in the Navy, where he became a Captain. They also throw some light on his crutches. He was severely wounded in the leg in the engagements with the Dutch off Portland, 18–20 February 1653, and before the Texel at the end of the following July. From 1655 to 1657 as Captain of the *Lizard* he was engaged in convoying English ships. His taking of the Dutch East Indiaman *Morning Star* as a prize almost became an international incident. His conversion to Quakerism must have occurred about August 1657 when a new commander suddenly appears on the *Lizard* and assurance is given that none of its company 'are tainted with Quakerism'. The following May he is suffering the first of his many imprisonments as a Quaker. In 1659, writing from Newgate to the Mayor and Recorder of London, he speaks of his earlier life (and wounds) as follows:

'Friends know that I am a man free-born in this Nation (the land of my nativity) and have faithfully served my generation in the late wars and commotions from time to time against the common enemies, namely the Kings, the Dutch, the Portugal, French and Spaniard; and what I have from time to time suffered, at present I mention little; besides the wounds and shedding of my blood, with my bones shot and shattered to pieces, and taken out of my body; And there was a time and times also in the behalf of the Nation, I could say to one, go, and he goeth, and to ten, come, and it was so; and to a hundred, do this and that, and it was done: but this is past away

55 c There was a woman...on crutches*...and was healed.

56 a And when G.F. was...sick*...at Lancaster prison.

56 b John Saker, who liveth in L...distracted*... good [.] cheerfully.

56 c And about 1667 when...fever*...the man's name was Gibbons*.

---

as the dust before the wind, etc.' (*The Prophet Approved*, etc. published by Thomas Hart, p. 1).

In his later life he returned to the sea, and is said to have died at sea. In 1679 he and three of his sons were 'taken captive by the Turk' (letter of Roger Longworth, Pemberton MSS. I, 126), but he was apparently redeemed by Friends.

In 1661 when Baker visited Malta and offered his own life for the release of Katharine Evans and her companion from the Inquisition there, Katharine writes to her husband that his 'outward being is near London'. The few references to him in London Quaker records do not enable us to place his home more exactly.

55 c This entry was doubtless suggested by the preceding since both were cases on crutches. Like no. 55 b also this may be a doublet. See the account in no. 35 b and p. 59 of the lame woman cured at William Dewsbury's house.

56 a For Fox's imprisonment at Lancaster in 1664–5, see no 55 a.

56 b Probably John Sagar of Marsden, Lancs (1627–1707) is intended whose sufferings in Lancashire between 1656 and 1689 are detailed by Besse, and are noted in part in II, 71, and more fully in Lancaster MSS. 3. Perhaps the miracle related here was not a cure, but the fact that this Friend suffered *cheerfully* the spoiling of his *goods*, even though this and other punishments of his drove his wife *distracted*. Besse, *Suff.*, vol. I, p. 317, writes under the year 1668: 'John Sagar prosecuted in the Ecclesiastical Court for tithes, was excommunicated for not appearing there at a time when he was close shut up in goal, and in consequence of that excommunication was detained in prison four years and an half. His wife, afflicted at the loss of her husband, and the difficulty of supporting four children in his absence, became distracted. The prosecutor would not permit him the liberty of so much as once visiting his wife in that doleful condition.' A biographical sketch is in *Piety Promoted*, pt. IV.

56 c Also spelled Gibbins. These surnames as well as Gibbon appear in early Quaker records. As an example of the latter we may mention one, who like Daniel Baker (no. 55 b) was a maimed veteran, 'Matthew Gibbon, of Molton in the County of Glamorganshire, formerly a Captain, who in the

56 *d*   And at Canterbury...sick*...herself and others.

56 *e*   In the 3rd month 1674 G.F. went to...sick*... anatomy*...that came to see her.

56 *f*   There was a young woman...headache*... according to her faith.

56 *g*   G.F. coming from London...King's-evil*... blessed be his name.

57 *a*   G.F. was had to a man...London*...leg*...and he praised God.

57 *b*   Ellen (*v.* Helen) Dundas* her desire of Margaret F[ell]...gout*...how she mended.

57 *c*   Upon the 20th of 4th month 1676 Rachel Yeamans*...giveth and taketh.

---

service of the Commonwealth had lost the use of one arm' (Besse, *Suff.*, vol. I, p. 740; *Abstract*, vol. I, p. 273; cf. Swarthmore MSS. IV, 219, quoted in M. E. Hirst, *The Quakers in Peace and War*, p. 56). Fox was in Wales for an extended visit in 1667.

56 *d*   Fox records in his *Journal* visits to Canterbury in 1655 and 1670. Cf. nos. 43 *a* and 43 *b* (Kent).

56 *e*   In May ('third month') 1674 between the sessions at Worcester in April and those in July Fox had some freedom, travelling to London where he appeared before the Judges at Westminster. He attended London Yearly Meeting in that month also.

56 *g*   Probably the same case as is described in no. 27 *a*. See the account quoted there from II, 310, and the note. The cure had taken place on a previous visit. This paragraph described perhaps the report of its success which Fox received on his way from London to Swarthmore in 1675.

57 *b*   On Helen Dundas, wife and later widow of William Dundas, see *Household Account Book*, p. 569. There can be no doubt that she was a widow at the time to which that note refers (1676). For other references, see *Annual Catalogue*, index. In 1678–9 she is greeted by Fox in letters sent to Robert Barclay in Scotland. According to Fox's unpublished history of Friends written in 1689 William Dundas and Helen his wife declared the Truth in France and spread books until they were not able to bear them. Cf. II, 429 f. Their home was near Edinburgh. In the present entry the name is given once as Ellen and once as Helen. As there is no date for this entry in the 'Book of Miracles', one cannot tell whether to expand MF as Margaret Fell or as Margaret Fox.

57 *c*   According to an entry in her own copy-book still extant, Rachel, daughter of William and Isabel (*née* Fell) Yeamans, died the following day: 'R.Y. deceased about the 5th hour in the morning upon the 21 day of the

57 d   Upon the 5th day of the week...Thomas Lower*
...birth*...temple to dwell in.

58 a   And there was a young woman...blind*...
belonging to Margaret Walker*.

58 b   And so the same spirit of intercession...Derby*
prison...birth*...the Lord is revealed.

60 a   And there was a captain...crutches*...more to
this day.

4th month being the 4th day of the week 1676' (see II, 410; *Household
Account Book*, p. 562). Fox was at Swarthmore Hall at the time and was
doubtless called in to help. The full story may have been similar to no. 66 b.
The last words at least, echoing Job i. 21: 'The Lord gave and the Lord hath
taken away, blessed be the name of the Lord', show that it ended on the
same note. Her parents were married in 1664 and had lost at least two other
children before this, in 1666 and 1674 (II, 410). The *Household Account Book*
kept by her aunt Sarah Fell at Swarthmore mentions three weeks before the
child's death a pint of brandy bought 'for cousin [i.e. niece] Rachel
Yeamans when she was not well', and three days after her death a sum of
£2. 7s. 3d. given to the poor at her funeral. The name is regularly spelled
in the Index to the Annual Catalogue 'Yeomans'.

57 d   On Thomas Lower, son-in-law of Margaret Fell, see I, 440, and
below no. 61 e.

58 a   Among the names of Cumberland women protesting against tithes
in 1659 occur three Margaret Walkers (*These Several Papers*, pp. 9, 15, 17).
Among sufferers Besse, *Suff.*, mentions a Margaret Walker in Durham
or Northumberland 1683 (I, 187) and a Margaret Walker of Sedbridge
(Sedbergh?) Meeting, Yorkshire, in 1671 (II, 136). There is no way to identify
the person here named. A Margaret Walker of Dacre, Greystoke Parish,
Cumberland, was disowned by Friends in connection with a lawsuit about
1673, and in 1675 with her husband, Edward Walker, was excommunicated
by the Church (*J.F.H.S.* (1909), vol. VI, pp. 150–2).

58 b   Another paragraph (no. 35 a) also connected with Fox's imprisonment in 1650 at Derby deals with a child's birth, perhaps the same incident.

60 a   In spite of the fact that Daniel Baker's crutches are twice mentioned
elsewhere (nos. 55 b, 65 a-b) it is not impossible that this paragraph too refers
to him. At any rate we know that he had been captain of a ship of war. See
Extracts from State Papers, pp. 45 f. and on no. 55 b. For the mention of
crutches compare the early hostile account of Fox commanding a cripple to
throw away his crutches, above, p. 21, and Dewsbury's account of a lame
woman cured by Friends, p. 59, whose ending may be compared with the
words above: '...having no need of crutches any more'.

60 b   And in 1652 there was...Colonel West* a justice
...sick*...the power of God.

And Colonel West stood up who had long been weak and blessed
the Lord and said he never saw so many sober people and good
faces together all the days of his life, and said that the Lord had
healed him that day, and said, 'George, if thou hast anything to
say to the people thou mayest freely declare it in the open sessions.'

I, 70 (Lancaster, 1652)

60 c   And at Bristol there was...sick*...she was
healed.

60 d   And Colonel Benson* a justice of the (peace)...
dying*...called it mine.

60 e   George Quilter* who liveth...gout*...to his
glory.

61 a   Richard Crowly*ʹ his wife...king's-evil*...and
gladness, etc.

61 b   And also after this G.F....distracted*...settled
her mind, etc.

---

60 b   On Colonel William West, see I, 412. The same incident is related
also by Fox as follows but without the name: 'And one of the justices said
he never saw such a day in his life, for he had been sick and that day he was
made whole' (III, 27). The date of the hearing at which Judge West made
this statement is calculated to be 18 October 1652 according to Braithwaite,
Beginnings, p. 107.

60 d   On Justice or Colonel Gervase Benson, see no. 21 b and note.

60 e   According to the registers of Thaxted Monthly Meeting George and
Frances Quilter lived at Saling Parva in Essex, where children were born to
them in 1651, 1653 and 1662. Frances Quilter died in 1668. Her name is
included among the 7000 women Friends who signed *These Several Papers
against Tithes* (1659), p. 37 (Essex).

61 a   A Richard Crowley of Leicestershire, perhaps of Leicester, is
mentioned by Besse, *Suff.*, vol. I, pp. 342, 344, as having goods distressed
in 1682 and 1684. He is perhaps the Richard Crauley whose marriage in
1667 to Katern Shellington was listed on folio 10 in the old register of
Leicester Monthly Meeting according to the index to that book (consulted
for me by Mr A. W. Read).

61 b   With the concluding phrase compare no. 17. Possibly this episode
is the one of the woman at Chichester (I, 201) quoted under no. 65 e. It
uses the same terms 'distracted' and 'settled her mind'.

61 *c*   One Major Beard's* wife...not well*...other times, etc.

61 *d*   And after G.F. came into...Raner*...persecutor*...interest to boot, etc.

---

61 *c*   Major Robert Beard of Essex appears as early as October 1649 in the *Calendar of Proceedings of the Committee for the Advance of Money, 1642–1656*, p. 1149. From the *Calendar of State Papers* we learn that on 31 January 1650 a commission was granted to Major Robert Beard to command a regiment of foot for the Western Division of Essex (1649–50, p. 499) and a little later to be Lieutenant-Colonel (1650, p. 504). From April to September 1651 he was Captain of one troop of the Second Horse Regiment for London and Kent (1651, pp. 514, 444, 442). In 1659 Major Beard is mentioned by Steven Crisp as a Friend of Essex and as one of those fit for appointment as Justice of the Peace for that County (*Extracts from State Papers Relating to Friends*, p. 106). A general meeting of Friends at Major Beard's apparently in London is mentioned by Fox in 1660 at the time of the Fifth Monarchy uprising (I, 386). Ellwood's substitution of the indefinite 'a Friend's house' may indicate that the Major left the Society. Robert Beard (without Major) is among the names given by Besse, *Suff.*, of Quakers persecuted at Evesham in 1655 (II, 56), at Sawbridgeworth, Herts, in 1659 (I, 241), and at Ratcliff, London, in 1684 (I, 471). It was not unusual for Friends to use military titles in speaking of their fellow members and Fox does so of persons long after they have left the army. See III, 372, *J.F.H.S.* vol. XXIV, p. 55 n., vol. xxvi, p. 51, and in the 'Book of Miracles', nos. 60 *a*, 60 *b*, 60 *d*, and, for persons not known to have been Friends, ibid. nos. 8 and 10 *b*.

More is known of Nicholas Beard, an early convert in Sussex, and his wife Susanna. He is mentioned in Fox's *Journal*, I, 184, though 'Major Beard' was written there first and then corrected.

The ending probably said that on recovery she was as well as at other times. So an account by William Penn of an Indian chief who when sick first sweat himself to a great fire and then plunged himself in the cold river ends: '...and then he rose, and fell to getting us our dinner, seeming to be as easy and well in health, as at any other time.' (Letter to the author in Edward Baynard, ψυχρολουσία, *or the History of Cold Bathing* (3rd ed. 1709), p. 289.)

61 *d*   Apparently not a cure but one of the judgements upon persecutors, or escapes from persecutors, which was included in the 'Book of Miracles'. Cf. nos. 73 *a*, 73 *b*, 73 *c*, 75 *b*. Among the early writers against Quakerism were Rev. Edward Reyner of Lincoln and John Reyner, his son (Smith, *Bibliotheca Anti-Quakeriana*, p. 378). There was a John Reyner, who while 'priest' at Dover, New Hampshire (1655–69) vigorously opposed Friends (see Besse, Whiting, etc.).

61 *e*   I, G.F., coming out of the S[outh]...Thomas Lower*...birth*...and obey him.

61–2   Dear and tender friend,
My dear little...Thomas Lower*...sick*...according to her faith.

62 *a*   I, John Banks* of Cumberland,...hand*...forever more. Amen.

---

61 *e*   Thomas Lower is named also in the next item, as well as earlier (no. 57 *d*). There is no evidence that in any of these passages it was Lower himself that was sick, though his serious illness at London with a fever and ague just before his marriage to Mary Fell in 1668 is known to us from a letter of Tho. Salthouse to Margaret Fell (Swarthmore MSS. I, 103) printed in part in L. V. Hodgkin, *A Quaker Saint of Cornwall* (1927), p. 210. For various infant deaths and illnesses in the family, see ibid. p. 144.

61–2   For the ending compare no. 37 *d*.

62 *a*   On John Banks (spelled in the index either Bankes or Bancks, cf. II, 325, Banckes), see II, 466 f. The incident is told by John Banks himself under the year 1677 as follows (*Journal of John Banks* (1712), pp. 66–7):

'About this time, a pain struck into my shoulder, which gradually fell down into my arm and hand, so that the use thereof I was wholly deprived of; and not only so, but my pain greatly increased both day and night; and for three months I could neither put my clothes on nor off myself, and my arm and hand began to wither, so that I did seek to some physicians for cure, but no cure could I get by any of them; until at last, as I was asleep upon my bed, in the night time, I saw in a vision, that I was with dear George Fox; and I thought I said unto him, "George, my faith is such, that if thou seest it thy way to lay thy hand upon my shoulder, my arm and hand shall be whole throughout."

'Which remained with me after I awaked, two days and nights (that the thing was a true vision) and that I must go to G.F. until at last, through much exercise of mind, as a near and great trial of my faith, I was made willing to go to him; he being then at Swarthmore, in Lancashire, where there was a meeting of Friends, being on the first day of the week. And some time after the meeting, I called him aside into the hall, and gave him a relation of my concern as aforesaid, showing him my arm and hand; and in a little time, we walking together silent, he turned about, and looked upon me, lifting up his hand, and laid it upon my shoulder, and said, "The Lord strengthen thee both within and without." And so we parted, and I went to Thomas Lower's of Marsh Grange that night; and when I was sate down to supper in his house, immediately, before I was aware, my hand was lifted up to do its office, which it could not for so long as aforesaid; which struck me into a great admiration, and my heart was broke into true tenderness before the Lord, and the next day I went home, with my hand and arm

62 *b*   And Jane Cowell* of Ulverston...hand*...her belief, well.

62 *c*   And at another time she [Jane Cowell*] was... fever*...praise of the Lord.

62 *d*   Likewise the said Jane Cowell* had a c[hild]... flux*...gladding of the mother.

63 *a*   Isabel Yeamans* and three maids...sick*...and mended all.

63 *b*   At London John Langstaff* was...sick*...glory for ever. Amen.

63 *c*   Mary Foster* who lives in L[ondon]...sick*... to the praise of the Lord.

---

restored to its former use and strength, without any pain. And the next time that G.F. and I met he readily said, "John, thou mended, thou mended"; I answered, "Yes, very well, in a little time." "Well," said he, "give God the glory."'

62 *b*   For Jane Holme who became the wife of John Cowell of Ulverston in 1665, see *Household Account Book*, pp. 515 and 528. There was another Jane Cowell, wife of John Cowell of Ulverston in the preceding decade. These three entries in the 'Book of Miracles' probably refer to one person, but it is hard to say which one.

63 *a*   For Isabel Fell, daughter of Margaret Fell, see II, 492. In 1664 she married William Yeamans, merchant of Bristol, who died in 1674. Her daughter Rachel is the subject of another item in this book (no. 57 *c*). There is an article on Isabel Yeamans in *J.F.H.S.* (1915), vol. XII, pp. 53–8, including references to her four delicate children. Only the boy William, born in 1669, survived childhood.

63 *b*   For John Langstaff of Bishop Auckland, see II, 478. A variant account of his conversion to Quakerism attributes it to the visit of Ann Audland in 1654. He had considerable eminence in the county, not only among Friends but in the community. Quaker meetings were held regularly at his house at Shakerton from 1671 to 1673. He is certainly to be identified with the contractor and builder of the same name. See *The Langstaffs of Teesdale and Weardale* (1906) by George B. Longstaff. Quaker records indicate that he was in London in May 1673 when he was a signer of the Yearly Meeting Epistle, and probably at other times.

63 *c*   On Mary Foster, see no. 15 *b*. The present tense of the verb 'lives' dates the writing of this paragraph before her death in 1686.

63 d And G.F. likewise came...Catharine Whaley*...
not well*...Witness, Thomas Dockray.

63 e Ellinor Claypool* wife of J[ames]...breast*...
it broke and mended.

63 f When G.F. was in Wales...fever*...name for
ever. Amen.

64 a The testimony of Mary Elson*...weak*...to the
glory of God.

64 b Agnes Pool* her testimony...toothache*...his
power for ever. Amen.

65 a–b And there was a man...tailor*...bed-
ridden*...
And Daniel Baker* who went...crutches*...never wore
them afterward.

---

63 d Catharine Whaley is not identified. Friends of the same surname
lived in Lancashire, Yorkshire, etc. On Thomas Dockray, see II, 488; III,
352; *Household Account Book*, p. 573. He was with Fox in London in 1678
(III, 272 f.) and in 1679 wrote for him at Swarthmore. This event evidently
belongs to some time or place of the association of Fox and Dockray. For
the use of witnesses' signatures, see above, p. 73.

63 e On James and Helena Claypoole of London, see III, 296. The spelling
Ellinor used by the indexer is evidently interchangeable with Helena.
Compare variants in no. 57 b.

64 a On John and Mary Elson (Nelson) of the Peel, Clerkenwell, London,
see II, 433, 457, 493; III, 295.

64 b Agnes Pool was a member of the Elson family in London. See
Annual Catalogue, 17, 49 F. She is mentioned also in Besse, *Suff.*, vol. I,
p. 365, as suffering imprisonment in London in 1659. In the same year her
name occurs in the list for London and Southwark of *These Several Papers
against Tithes* (p. 55).

An Agnes Pool is mentioned in 1671 as appointed with Mary Foster and
some men Friends in connection with the sufferings of Friends in London
(*Sundry Ancient Epistles*, p. 40). She is a signer of an undated paper issued
by the Box Meeting, and of the following printed items: *A Tender and
Christian Testimony...from our Women's-Meeting at the Bull and Mouth*
(1685), *Piety Promoted by Faithfulness* (a testimony to Ann Whitehead,
1686).

65 a–b As elsewhere the index has combined two items. On Daniel
Baker and his lameness, see above, no. 55 b. Probably the 'went' was not
followed by a place-name but is used idiomatically 'went on crutches'.

65 c   Margaret Drinkwell* of Lo[ndon] was very s[ick] ...sick*...and praise for ever.

65 d   Humphrey Scott* of Riston in Yo[rkshire]... sick*...dying*...he being a tailor.

65 e   G.F. went into Sussex*...distracted*...before distraction was.

And the woman of the house, though she was convinced she fell into love with one of the world who was there at that time. And after I took her aside and was moved to pray for her and to speak to her and a light thing got up in her and she slighted it. And after she married this man of the world she went distracted for he was greatly in debt. And I was sent for to her and the Lord raised her up again and settled her mind by his power. And after her husband died, and she acknowledged the just judgments of God was come upon her for slighting my exhortations when I prayed for her.

I, 201 (Chichester, Sussex, 1655)

66 a   Anne Robinson...Lydia Oades*...ulcer*...back again well.

---

65 c   On Margaret Drinkwell, whose house was in Bishopsgate Street, parish of Shoreditch, see II, 385; III, 311. She died in 1695 aged 72 years. According to a letter she wrote to Margaret Fell in 1662 (Swarthmore MSS. I, 367) she was born within ten miles of the Isle of Ely.

65 d   Rylstone in Yorkshire is the name of a place which early received the Quaker message. See *F.P.T.* Humphrey Scott is not identified from Quaker records. But the Parish Register, which is printed and indexed, fortunately listed some burials of Friends. Five such are noted under the year 1658 including 'Humfrid Scot May 31 age 37 at Rilston 4 [i.e. fourth burial there this year] a quaker, reakes.' The christening of 'Humfrid [son of] William Scot, Sept 14', 1623 is also mentioned by the 'priest' for that time, John Toppan. *The Register of St Peter's, Rylstone (formerly part of the Ancient Parish of Burnsall)*, edited by C. H. Lowe (Leeds, 1895), pp. 60 and 112. Rilston Raikes (or Reakes) is the name of an old Quaker burying-ground. Though long disused and without any marks of burials, it has survived to modern times a little plot about 13 square yards with an old gateway (ibid. p. iv). Humphrey Scott's early death dates this cure within a few years; it explains also the absence of his name in later Quaker records. In 1668 Rylstone is included in Scalehouse Meeting (*J.F.H.S.* (1905), vol. II, p. 35).

66 a   On Lydia Oades of London, see III, 333. Her name first occurs in the 1659 protest against tithes (*These Several Papers*, p. 55). Anne Robinson and Lydia Oades visited Jamaica in January 1662 (Portfolio 17-2; cf. *J.F.H.S.* (1913), vol. X, pp. 118, 121), together with Oswell Heritage and John

66 *b*   And on the second day [of the night I hearing that Margaret Rouse's* child was sick I went to see it and as I stood by it considering its condition I felt the Lord's power to go through it, and the words was, 'The Lord's power was come to raise it up or to fetch it away.' And so I came away fresh in the Lord's power and was satisfied in myself.

And the next day her mother came to the town and desired me to go with her and see it, and through her tenderness I went though I was satisfied in myself. And so I saw the child was full of the power of the Lord and it rested upon it and rested in it. And at night it died.

And after the spirit of the child appeared to me and there was a mighty substance of a glorious life in that child

---

Taylor. The last-named writes in his *Journal* (1710, p. 19; 1830, p. 35 f.): 'Two of my Friends (viz. Anne Robinson and Oswell Heritage) were very sick and weak of the country distemper and they both died and so finished their course and testimony for the Truth in that Island. They were honest women and the Lord's power was with them to the last.' Lydia Oades 'was a very sweet quiet spirited woman too, and the Lord's power was with her and she had good service for Truth in many places and countries and lived to come for Old England to her dear husband and children again to her great joy and comfort in the Lord'. If the 'Book of Miracles' dealt with this association of the two women that it mentioned, I think the cure was that of Lydia Oades and that the last words refer to her return to England.

66 *b*   This paragraph was apparently taken entire from a rough draft of the *Journal* of Fox now preserved at London (see *Annual Catalogue*, 19, 90 G), as 73 *c*, 75 *a* and 75 *b* were taken from the *Itinerary Journal* for 1683.

Bridget Rous, daughter of John and Margaret (*née* Fell) Rous, died of the small-pox on 30th of 11 mo. 1682/3 in the parish of Stepney and was buried at Chequer Alley later called Bunhill Fields.

Visits to young Margaret Rous, a sister of the above, during illnesses are mentioned by Fox in 10 mo. 1683 (III, 89; Ellwood, 1694, p. 519; 1891, II, 396), in 9 mo. 1685 (III, 126; 1694, p. 535; 1891, II, 418). Note two small additions of Ellwood in these places: in the first 'and had a desire to see me', in the second 'but recovered'. This and the following three items seem to make a series of four episodes connected with Margaret Rous (the elder). On her, see II, 421.

With this reassuring appearance to Fox of the deceased compare no. 11 *b*, and also the following from his Derby imprisonment in 1650–1: 'And two men suffered for small things and I was moved to admonish them for their theft, to encourage them concerning their suffering, it being contrary to the

and I bid her mother be content, for it was well, and it was
well that she had such an innocent offering for the Lord.
And she was finely settled and contented through the will]
of the Lord.   11 mo. 29–30, 1682 (Jan. 1683)

66 *c*   And after her (Margaret Rouse's*) daughter...
smallpox*...and do well

67 *a*   And Margaret Rouse came...Fretwell*...sick...
small pox*...recover and was well.

67 *b*   And in her house...Blackamoor*...full of the
small pox*.

67 *c*   There came two women* to...temptation*...
to the Lord for ever.   Amen.

---

law of God, and a little after they had suffered their spirits appeared to me as
I was walking and I saw the men was well' (I, 14, not in Ellwood). Compare
also the language of Fox's letter to Robert and Jane Widders upon the
death of their son: 'Be content in the will of God; and take all for good at
the hand of the Lord, and what he doth; for thy son is well, and in rest and
peace...' (Swarthmore, 16th of 5 mo. 1676, *Annual Catalogue*, 82 F).

66 *c*   Compare note on 66 *b*. It is possible that the smallpox mentioned
here was not that of the Rous daughter or of the servant (cf. 67 *b*), but of
the son, Nathaniel Rous. He had the 'fluxing pox' in March 1685/6 but was
not very sick and recovered (III, 134). Cf. Helen Crosfield, *Margaret Fox*
(1913), p. 207.

67 *a*   The name Fretwell was found among Friends in England including
London, where Margaret and John Rous lived. There was, however, a more
prominent family of Fretwells in Barbados, and since Margaret Rous visited
that island where her father-in-law lived, in 1678 and perhaps earlier (II,
421), this episode may well belong there.

67 *b*   A negro would be much more likely to be mentioned together with
Margaret Rous in Barbados (see no. 67 *a*) than in London, though on account
of her husband's connections with the former they may have had a negro
servant in England. I do not know of any references to negroes among
Friends in England in the period. Fox's suggestion that one be sent to him
was apparently playful, and we do not know that it was carried out. See his
Gospel Family Order (1676), p. 22, and the unpublished reference in a later
letter: 'And as for sending over a negro to me (it is no matter) I did it
but to try them.' MS. at Friends' House, London (marked L in *Annual
Catalogue*, p. 2), p. 343.

67 *c*   What is preserved of this item raises the suspicion that it was not
a typical miracle story. But it is just possible it is the episode of two or

68   In the 9th month 1685 Mary Stale* the jo...
measles*...Lord had the glory.

69 *a*   John Loung's* wife was sick of...fever*...
Tr[uth] of God to this day.

69 *b*   And there was another woman...London*...
fever*...is well to this day.

69 *c*   Esther Biddle* who followed the pr[...]s that
received...of the deaf* to his honour.

70 *a*   In Enemessex* in Maryland...moping*...had
been among them.

And there was a woman at Anamessicks which had been many
years in trouble and would sometimes sit moping near two months

---

three women who came to Thomas Atkins' wife to secure her help for a
seriously afflicted Presbyterian woman near Nailsworth related by Fox (see
above, p. 10).

68   Mary Stale is not identified. Fox's own activities during 9th month
1685 are fully given for the first 17 days, including visits to Bridget (Austill ?)
who was sick at South Street, and to young Margaret Rous, who was sick
at Kingston. The rest of the month he lived at the Rous home (III, 125 f.).

69 *a*   Neither the individual nor even the surname is identified. I suspect
the latter is not right, but it is unmistakably written so in the MS index.

69 *c*   On Esther (Hester) Biddle, see I, 459. Unfortunately the abbreviation is not clear enough to be resolved. Apparently the last phrase referred
to God who opens the ears 'of the deaf to his honor' and implies that this was
the cure wrought upon (or by) Esther Biddle. According to Fox (II, 334, 336)
she went in 1656 to Newfoundland and in 1657 to Barbados. Her travels and
travails in England are represented by the references in Besse, *Suff.*, vol. I,
pp. 366, 484, 564, 689. Her record as a Friend in Holland was not a very
favourable one, to judge from William I. Hull, *Willem Sewel of Amsterdam*,
pp. 129 f.; *The Rise of Quakerism in Amsterdam*, pp. 283 f., 305. Her travels
may have included a journey to Gibraltar, if that is what 'the Straites'
means in a letter from William Caton of 1661 (Swarthmore MSS. I, 415),
and later, if Croese's statement is to be believed (*General History of the
Quakers* (Engl. tr. 1696), pp. 267 ff.; cf. Keith's caveat, ibid. Appendix IX,
pp. 23 f.), a dramatic peace mission to King Louis XIV of France in person.
In connection with a child born to them in 1668 that died in 1670 the
Friends' registers refer to her husband, Thomas Biddle, as a shoemaker and
their residence as in Barnaby Street, Southwark, in the Parish of (St)
Magdalen, Bermondsey.

70 *a*   Apparently a doublet of no. 21 *a*.

together and hardly speak nor mind anything. So I was moved to go to her and tell her that salvation was come to her house, and did speak other words to her and for her. And that hour she mended and passed up and down with us to meetings and is well. Blessed be the Lord!

II, 243 (Anamessicks, Maryland, 3rd of 1 mo. 1673)

70 *b*   And after a men and women's meeting... woman*...ulcer*...through her and changed her.

71 *a*   In 1683 there was a young woman*...fever*... well, blessed be the Lord.

71 *b*   About that time there was...woman*...weak* ...have the praise and glory.

73 *a*   Chrysilla Grice* said that after she w...persecutor*...Fox*...dagger*...so spoken against them.

---

70 *b*   Ulcers are mentioned also in nos. 21 *c*, 45 *a* and 66 *a*. Without claiming its identity we may cite here the story which G. Croese, *General History* (Engl. tr. 1696), p. 28, says that Fox's friends told of him: 'that having ended his discourse to the people, he happened once to meet with a woman (accompany'd by her husband) all over scabby, ulcerous and covered round with cataplasms; upon which he enquired of the husband if he had the faith of miracles; but while he was hesitating, and delaying to answer, he asked the same question of the woman, and she having answered affirmatively, he immediately pull'd off the cataplasms, and she was forthwith restored to her health'.

71 *a*   In spite of the full, almost daily, entries in the extant *Journals* of Fox for much of the year 1683 (III, 77–90), the young woman with fever is not to be identified.

73 *a*   This episode, together with the next three following, appears to belong with escapes from persecutors or with judgements on persecutors— categories found occasionally in the 'Book of Miracles'—rather than with cures of disease. The name Chrysilla Grice is confirmed by an entry in the *Annual Catalogue*, 5, 65 G. That was a letter written to her by Fox in March 1678 about her young man or son that 'he may spend the little time he hath to the Glory of God'. Peel Monthly Meeting recorded that on 14 April 1670 Aristotle Grice, son of Grissel, died of a consumption in their home in the parish of Giles Cripplegate, London, and was buried at Chequer Alley. Evidently the mother of these two boys is the same and was the subject of this passage in the 'Book of Miracles'. Other references to her have been sought in vain. Is her husband John Grice of New Cheapside, Moorfields, whose two-weeks old daughter was buried in the same burial place in 1669? The surname Grice occurs later in the registers for Cheshire and for Southwark. An Emanuel Grice from Durham is frequently mentioned as a sufferer in Besse.

73 *b*   And there was a woman...opposers*...tongue*
...to her dying day.

73 *c*   [A Short account of the persecutors* of Ringwood*
in Hampshire.]

There was a meeting [intended by the people of God
called Quakers at Poulner* in the parish aforesaid in the
year 1663 on the last day of the 3rd month. Before the
meeting was gathered and the hour was come that the
meeting was appointed, John Line, constable, came with
John Street, captain of the train bands, with soldiers and
took 17 men, and after those men were hailed away there

---

73 *b*   Perhaps this is not a cure, but one of the judgements upon
persecutors which got into the 'Book of Miracles' instead of the 'Book of
Examples'. Cf. note on no. 61 *d*. The victims of such punishments often
suffered in the tongue, by poetic justice, as in III, 36: 'one used to hold out
his tongue at Friends when they went by them, and he died with his tongue
hanging out of his mouth below his chin'. Cf. I, 149, 348.

The last cited passage, a separate sheet which I suspect is really also from
the 'Book of Examples', is inserted in Ellwood at a little different place
under the year 1659 (p. 206). It tells of a man who 'played pranks' at the
Quakers' general meeting 'with a bear skin upon his back'. He stood
opposite the Friend that was speaking 'with his tongue lolling out of his
mouth' but on his way home at a bull-baiting 'the bull struck his tongue out
of mouth which hung lolling out of his mouth as he had used in derision
before'. A similar if not identical story is related independently in Besse,
Abstract of Sufferings, vol. I, p. 80; *Suff.*, vol. I, pp. 165 f.; Edward
Billing, *Word of Reproof*, p. 94, and the place is given as Evershot (Dorset),
the wicked man as Thomas Hurlston(e), the Quaker speaker as John Scafe,
the date as 1656, the cloak as a bull-skin, and the death a few months after.

The same motif of poetic justice in the same form occurs in the preceding
reference (I, 149) at Halifax in 1654. 'And another of the butchers aforesaid
that had sworn to kill me, that used to put his tongue out of his mouth to
Friends when they went by him, he died with his tongue so swollen out of
his mouth that he could not get it into his mouth again till he died.' Of
another opponent we are told: 'The judgments of God that overtook the
persecutors of James Parnell were very remarkable. Dionysius Wakering,
that pretended to arrest him in the name of Oliver Cromwell, Protector,
was taken with the smallpox, his tongue being very much swelled in his
head, saying, "Oh! this Parnell. Oh! that I had never meddled with this
Parnell," and so died.' (*F.P.T.* p. 97.)

73 *c*   See notes in III, 298 f. numbered 80, 1–3 and 80, 4. The Hampshire
Friends records of deaths mention all the victims here named as members
at Ringwood until the time of their death, mostly early in the eighteenth
century. Elizabeth Bemister, of Ringwood, as appears to be her right name,

was a meeting held by G.F. The known persecutors were Thomas Blackherd, warden, John Line, constable, John Street, captain. And it was observed by many people that the evident hand of God fell upon them. All these were wealthy men and many did observe that the just hand of God was against them, as did plainly appear by their own confession, as also by the wasting of their outward estates.

The above said John Line, constable, carried these men to prison and when they were brought before the judges of the Assizes he took a false oath against them who were innocent, for which they were fined and kept prisoners more than ten years.

John Line, constable, died in the year 1682 a sad spectacle to behold; he grievously rotted away alive, and so died his wife also (being a persecutor) after the same manner or like example. And these things are generally known by the neighbourhood and witnessed by the sufferers, viz. Thomas Manner, Martin Bence, James Miller, Edward Pritchett, Philip Bence, etc. This John Line did confess that he never prospered since he laid hands on the Quakers, witnessed by John Chater who heard him speak the words with several others, and wished he had never meddled with them, and said he never prospered since, in the presence of Elizabeth Bannister, and said he was sorry he had a hand in persecuting the Quakers, and also that he would never meddle with them more, and said he thought the hand of the Lord was] against him for it.

III, 79 f., 1663

75 *a*   And on the 23rd of the 7th mo. '83 the constable [that plucked G. Fox* down made a confession and said, that day 7 weeks he had plucked G.F. down when he was

---

is likewise mentioned (ibid.). The non-Quaker records, civil and ecclesiastical, have not yet supplied further data on the persecutors. Fox describes his experience at this meeting in II, 24 f. and Elwood (1694), pp. 261 f.; (1891), II, 3–5.

75 *a*   Apparently the indexer once used the real ending of this piece, and once mistook for the ending the words 'to be penitent'. Such variations occur in earlier items in the 'Book of Miracles' and may have been due to

speaking, and since he had kept his bed within 4 days and he could hardly walk over the room, and his wife was sick at present and he had a pain in his back, shoulder and arm ever since, and he was loath to have been there but that he was forced and did not like that work. And some friends told him that he might hurt his back or shoulder by thrusting amongst the people and not by taking hold of G.F. But the constable answered and said he was smote and struck at the heart before he laid hands of G.F. to take him down. And so the constable seemed] to be penitent [and sorry, that he was brought into such a work and did not like it, and told the people what misery and trouble he had been in since] for meddling with Friends.

III, 81 f., London

75 b   And on the 25th day of the 1st month 1683 James Claypoole* [was mighty sick of the stone* that he could neither lie nor stand. He was in such extremity of the stone that he cried out like a woman in travail. And I went to him and spoke to him and was moved to lay my hand upon him and desired the Lord to rebuke his infirmity. And as I laid my hands upon him the Lord's power went through him. And his wife had faith and was sensible of the thing. And he presently fell off asleep and presently after his stone came from him like dirt and so then he was pretty well. Formerly he used to lie a month or two weeks of the stone, as he said, but the Lord's power in his time soon gave him ease, that he came the next day 25 miles] in a coach with me.

III, 78 (Worminghurst, Sussex)

---

a situation in the MS. exactly like that which we find in the printed edition III, 81, where the last words on the page are: 'And so the constable seemed to be penitent.' Only by turning the page does the reader find that the account continues three lines more until it ends with the words 'meddling with Friends'. This passage is indexed under 'Persecutor', but that word does not appear in the text.

75 b   This is the third successive passage in the 'Book of Miracles' derived from MSS. of the *Itinerary Journal* for 1683. This passage appears somewhat rewritten in Ellwood (1694, pp. 503 f.; 1891, II, 377 f.). For

76   I had a vision* that I was out of the body...over the tempter.

77 *a*   And there was a Friend...Nicholas Gates*... prince George* his child...fits*...that night did help it.

James Claypoole's own account of this visit, see above, pp. 58 f. For James Claypoole, see III, 296.

76   For other visions in the 'Book of Miracles', see nos. 25 and 9. Many visions are related in the *Journal* of Fox (II, 511, s.v. 'Visions'), but none of them appears to be the one here related. It may echo II Cor. xii. 1–7.

77 *a*   Nicholas Gates of Alton in Hampshire died in 1707 aged about 74 years. See the testimonies to him in his *Tender Invitation to All* (1708). There are various other references to him in Quaker sources both MS. and printed. The account in *Piety Promoted* is reprinted in *The Friend* (Philadelphia (1903), vol. LXXVI, p. 394). His connection with Friends went back to 1655.

Prince George of Denmark must be intended, whose wife, later Queen Anne of England, is said to have borne seventeen children. But only one of these survived babyhood. That was William Henry, Duke of Gloucester (1689–1700). He must be the child meant here. He was afflicted with attacks of ague and dizziness, was probably hydrocephalous, and was a cause of constant anxiety being delicate and abnormal as well as the precious heir-apparent.

As he was born in 1689 this reference to him gives us the latest datable event in the 'Book of Miracles'. Even if one of the older girls were intended, they both died 6 February 1687 aged 10 and 20 months respectively. That would imply a date later than no. 68.

Possibly the exact event mentioned here is recorded in a non-Quaker source in somewhat variant form. There again a Quaker is involved in connection with the fits of the prince and there again his improvement the following night is mentioned. But the Friend is not Nicholas Gates but a Mrs Pack or Peck as she is once called in the reprint. She is described as the wife of a Quaker who came from Kingston-Wick (a place near Worthing in Sussex). Her introduction to the Prince's household as wet-nurse is apparently to be dated in the late summer or autumn of 1689—the child was born 24 July—and to be placed at Hampton Court. She continued in the prince's service some time longer and is described as imperious and meddlesome, and extremely ugly. She finally retired on full salary of £40 a year. Through her intervention with the Queen she obtained for her husband a post in the Customs House, but she died soon after from smallpox. This was before October 1697 when Jenkin Lewis, another attendant of the little prince, left the service. To Lewis' intimate *Memoirs of William Henry, Duke of Glocester* (London, 1789), reprinted with notes by W. J. Loftie (London, 1881), under the title *Queen Anne's Son* we are indebted for these details. The episode most similar to the hints we have of that in the 'Book of Miracles' is told as follows (pp. 4–6, reprint, pp. 34–6):

'He was a very weakly child; and most people believed he would not live long: which is the less to be wondered at, as the Princess was breeding with

77 *b*   Mary Franklin* was very weak*...stomach to her meat.

78   And there was a man in Hertfordshire*...fever*... great while afterwards.

79   Widow Taylor* at Stoke in N[orfolk]...ague*... that believed in it.

---

him when, constrained by necessity, she took the painful journey alluded to, in the gloomy month of November, with dejected spirits and an aching heart. A Mrs. Shermon was chosen for his nurse; but her nipple proving too big, she was set aside for Mrs. Wanley, who had suckled a child of her Highness's before with good success, and therefore resumed the office of wet-nurse for six weeks, she being a handy, good-tempered woman. All people now began to conceive hopes of the Duke's living, when lo! he was taken with convulsion fits, which followed so quick one after another, that the physicians from London despaired of his life. They ordered change of milk; and nurses, with young children, came many at a time, several days together, from town, and the adjacent villages. There was a footman's wife, who belonged to Mrs. Ogle, a Maid of Honour to the Princess, who said her milk was younger than it proved to be; but Lady Charlotte Beverwort by examining the parish books, detected her in an untruth; she was therefore detained one night only. Fresh orders were given for nurses, and each gratified with five guineas. The Duke being given over by the physicians, all encouragement was offered for any one who could find a remedy for convulsion fits. Among the country women that attended, Mrs. Pack, the wife of a Quaker, came from Kingston-Wick, with a young child in her arms of a month old, to speak of a remedy which had restored her children. As she sat in the presence room, Prince George of Denmark happened to pass by; and observing her to be a strong, healthy woman, he ordered her to go to bed to the young prince, who soon sucked her, and mended that night, continuing well whilst she suckled him.'

77 *b*   Women named Mary Franklin are listed in Oxford in 1659 (*These Several Papers*, p. 46) and in Bristol in 1683 (Besse, *Suff.*, vol. I, p. 69, 'spinster'). The former may be either Mary Franklin of Witney who died in 1663, or the wife of Henry Franklin, who lived several decades later. See Oxfordshire Friends' registers. The phrase 'stomach to her meat' means 'appetite for her food' and is found elsewhere in Fox and in other contemporary writers.

79   A Stoke in Norfolk in the hundred of Clackclose is attested for the seventeenth century from various sources. See, for example, a *Book of the Names in England and Wales*, 1662, *Annual Catalogue*, 7, 42 G and 9, 10 G, letters addressed to Elizabeth Hubbard of Stoke, who with her husband is mentioned in Besse, *Suff.*, vol. I, p. 493, cf. p. 505. Also in *Extracts from State Papers*, p. 228, is a reference to John Hubbert (*sic*), Stoke, Norfolk, among dispersers of Quaker books. But no widow Taylor is known from Quaker sources.

INDEX

Figures in heavy face type indicate items actually occurring in the surviving text of the 'Book of Miracles'. They include with some additions the words which were cited in the old index and which are marked in this edition with an asterisk (see p. 100), except a few commoner terms like 'sick', 'not well', 'child', 'woman', etc.

Index

Index

Index

Farmer, Ralph, 6, 21
Farnsworth, Richard, 10, 34, 59
fasting, 5, 22, 32–6, 94, 121
Fell, Isabel, 138; *see also* Yeamans, Isabel
Fell, Leonard, **109**
Fell, Margaret, 13, 15, 45, 49, 51, 57, 129, **133**, 134; *see also* Fox, Mary
Fell, Margaret, the younger, 51, 125
Fell, Mary, 137; *see also* Lower, Mary
Fell, Sarah, 50, 134
Fenwick, John, 55
Fettiplace, Giles, 46
fever, 10 60, 69, **109**, **117**, **118**, **123**, **124**, **129**, **130**, **131**, **132**, **138**, **139**, **143**, **144**, **149**
Fifield, William, 8
Fifth Monarchy, 136
fire, calling down, 11
Firth, Charles H., 126
fish, draft of, 17, 18
fistula, 80
fits, convulsion, **127**, **148**
Florida, 72
Floyd, *see* Lloyd
flux, **138**
Foster, Mary, 64, **109**, **110**, **138**, 139
Foster, Matthew, lieut., 126
Fowler, Edward, bishop, 82
Fox, Christopher, 107
Fox, George, *passim*
  endorsements, 10, 13, 15, 27, 45
  writings:
    A Challenge to the Papists, 62
    A Few Words to all Such, 62
    A Reply to the Vindication, 86
    A Word from the Lord, 91
    An Answer to a Paper, 34–6
    'Book of Miracles', 38, 39, 40, 44, *et seq.*
    Concerning the Apostate Christians, 62
    Doctrinals, 97
    'Epistle to the Reader' in Josiah Coale's Works, 36
    Epistles, 42, 43, 70, 97, 101, 107
    Gospel Family Order, 142
    Haistwell Diary, 93

Here are Several Queries, 52
'How the Lord by his Power', etc., 38, 39, 122
Itinerary Journals, 46, 70, 141
Journal, passim
Short Journal, 38, 118
The Great Mistery, 24, 26, 27
Fox, Margaret, 17, 22, 133
Fox, Mary, **106–8**
France, 133, 143
Franck, Sebastian, x
Franeker, 31
Frankford, 70
Franklin, Henry, 149
Franklin, Mary, **149**
Frederickstadt, 93
Fretwell, ——, **142**
Fretwell, Ellen, 92
Friend(s), 9, **124**, **126**, **147**, **148**
Frith, Susan, 92
Furly, Benjamin, 54, 76
Furnace, Robert, 74

Gates, Nicholas, **148**
Gay, John, 110
Gell, Robert, 2, 61
George, Prince of Denmark, 67, **148**, 149
Gibbins, Gibbons, **132**; *see also* Gibbon
Gibbon, Matthew, capt., 132–3
Gibraltar, 143
Giles Cripplegate, 144
Glanvill, Joseph, 75, 81
Glasgow, 103
glister pipe, 50, 90
Gloucester, 103
Gloucester, William Henry, Duke of, 67, 68, **148**, 149
Gloucestershire, 16, **103**
gold, quintessence of, 67
goldsmith, **118**
gout, **133**, **135**
Graham, John W., 44
Grantham, Thomas, 26
Great Strickland, 48, 124
Greatrakes, Valentine, 12, 61, 73–5
Green, Joseph J., 54
Greene, Anne, 6
Greeneway, Sir Richard, 72

Index

Index

Index